# SEX WITH A MARRIED WOMAN

A Man's Guide to Loving His Wife

## Robert Mark Alter

(Author of *Good Husband, Great Marriage*)

Published by Merrimack Media
ISBN: 978-1-939166-03-6
Library of Congress Control Number: 1466472618
SKU: 51295
Manufactured in the United States of America, or in
Great Britain, when purchased outside of North or South America.

For further information, contact info@merrimackmedia.com

Cover design and illustration by Odessa Sawyer (www.OdessaSawyer.com)

# To my wife Jane

## From the sixties to our 60's
## still in love

*I loved her and sought her out from my youth*
*I desired to make her my spouse*
*and I was a lover of her beauty*
**– King Solomon**

*So she took her love for to gaze awhile*
*upon the fields of barley*
*In his arms she fell as her hair came down*
*among the fields of gold*
**– Sting**

# TABLE OF CONTENTS

# TABLE OF CONTENTS

# INTRODUCTION

*Let's talk about sex, baby*
*Let's talk about you and me . . .*
**– Salt 'n Pepa**

*Marriage is the perfection which love*
*aimed at.*
**– Ralph Waldo Emerson**

This book is about how a man can have great sex with a married woman, the girl of his dreams – his wife – all his life, in the marriage of his dreams.

Great sex in marriage? Are you kidding? Marital sex has such a bad reputation, especially among men, that the term "marital sex" is considered a contradiction in terms. The incompatibility of sex and marriage is a standing joke in movies, sitcoms, and comedy routines, and our society is replete with references to the inevitable monotony of sex in marriage or its complete disappearance. Zsa Zsa Gabor put it pretty succinctly in that sexy Hungarian voice of hers: "I know nothing about sex because I was always married." Everyone believes that great sex and long marriage don't go together – every Tom, Dick, and Harry – and Bill, and Mark, and John, and Anthony, and Eliot, and David, and Arnold, and Tiger – everyone thinks that marriage is the last place where you should expect to find great sex, and that if you want great sex, you better go outside the marriage for it.

But it's not true.

The truth is that marriage is the best sexual position there is. My goal in **SEX WITH A MARRIED WOMAN** is to restore the reputation of sex in marriage.

It won't be easy. My dentist showed me that.

I was at my dentist the other day for a checkup, and while he was getting his instruments set up he asked me when I was going to write another book. He had read and liked my previous book about husbanding, *Good Husband, Great Marriage* – his wife, he told me, kept leaving it on his pillow, propped open – and whenever I would come into his office, he would ask me about my writing.

"Actually, I *am* working on another book," I said.

"What's it about?" he said.

"Married sex," I said.

He paused and thought for a moment.

"Oh," he said, "a short book."

*******

It's true, this *is* a short book, but not because married sex has to be short or short-lived or so mechanical and predictable that there's not much to say about it. It's a short book because its message is short. And here's the message:

Sex between two married people who love each other does not have to be quick, cursory, meager, dull, or infrequent. Good, exciting sex doesn't have to disappear from a marriage with time. It doesn't have to do that after the first year of your marriage, or the first three years, or ten years, or the first thirty or forty years. The sex can be fun and frequent and thrilling all the way through – if you get the sex right – which means you have to get the marriage right.

What's more, a marriage between two people who love each other is the *best* place on the planet for sex because the best sex, the only *really* fun and exciting sex is between two people who love, know, and trust each other so much that they've surrendered everything to each other, and keep surrendering everything to each other for all the years of their lives, to have and to hold, their minds, hearts, souls, and bodies, and all their beautiful private places and the deepest, darkest secrets of their sexuality. That's a lot of surrender, and a lot of sexuality, and that's supposed to happen in your marriage.

This is very good news.

But there's a condition:

If you, the husband, give your wife what she, the woman, wants from you – which is caring, kindness, companionship, connection, attention, security, and fidelity – she will give you what you as a man want from her, which, give or take a few other things, is sex. If you become the husband she wants you to be – if you give her the love she wants from you in the forms she wants it – she, being a woman, will give you the love you want from her in the forms you want it. That includes the sexual form of her love. And not only will she give you sex, she'll *want* sex – with *you!* – a lifetime of *great* sex that will knock your socks off.

That's the message, and that's a lot of socks.

*******

For a man to give the love and connection and attention and

fidelity that his wife wants – to become the good and giving husband she wants so she'll be the good and giving wife *he* wants – takes discipline and work. Thank god that we men are good at discipline and work. One piece of the work is to come to understand your humanity and your masculinity and your sexuality and your marriage and your wife so deeply and to honor them all so highly that it becomes literally impossible for you to be a sexual man with a woman *other* than your wife. The other piece of the work is to learn everything that you, a man, can possibly learn about a woman's femininity and sexuality – what melts her heart and then all the rest of her – and so become a great lover to your wife. You'll learn about both pieces of the work in this book.

**SEX WITH A MARRIED WOMAN** is what I know about male sexuality, female sexuality, and marital sexuality. It's what I know about how to be a good and loving husband to your wife, how to fall so deeply into her good graces that she will welcome you with grace and love when you want to fall deeply into her arms. I've learned it all over the course of my thirty-six years talking to women and men as a psychotherapist and marriage counselor, and my forty-two years of marriage to my wife Jane.

To explain it all, I'll have to speak a little indelicately at times, for which I apologize to modest ears, and I'm going to have to say some hard, straight truths about the penis. I'm also going to joke about the sex in your marriage because if you can't joke about all the ins and outs and ups and downs of marital sex, what can you joke about? Don't get me wrong: I'm dead serious about sex – it plays a huge part in the body and psyche of a man and the health and happiness of a marriage and the life of the world – huge! – but it's hard – *very* hard – to be a man and talk deeply – *really* deeply – about sex for longer – *longer*! – than eight seconds without making the little sexual jokes and puns and innuendoes we men get a big kick out of snickering at – heh-heh – like Beavis and Butthead . . . beaver! – butt! – HEAD!! . . . so I do that sometimes, and I'll leave it to you to decide when I'm talking about sex with my tongue in my cheek, and when it's elsewhere.

The purpose of it all is to help men who want good sex in their marriages get it from their wives who want it too. The big message of **SEX WITH A MARRIED WOMAN** is that this can happen in your marriage because you, the husband, have it within your power to make it happen.

The kind of sex that you or any man is looking for outside your marriage in sexual dalliances, affairs, pornography, and all the other epidemic forms of adultery in this world can be found inside your marriage, with your wife, all your life – if you do your part. You have a part. **SEX WITH A MARRIED WOMAN** is the description of your part. Play it well, and then leave the rest to a wife (and a God) who loves you and wants you to be happy and likes sex and knows that sex makes you happy. Your part, in a word, is to become a good husband to your wife. That's your best shot at having a good marriage, and having a good marriage is your best shot at having a lifetime of great sex. Right now your part is simply to read the book you're holding in your hands, and everything follows from that.

It's an easy book to read. And a fun read. Logical. Helpful.

Straight at you. A man's kind of book. And like my dentist said, it's a short book, no wasted words, each chapter short, to the point, and fun, and you can basically chapter-surf your way through them the same way you channel-surf the TV, and have as good a time.

You're a man and a good man and a married man and you want to have sex with the woman you're married to. You want to have fun with your wife all your life. You want to know how you can *love* her.

Of course you do.

Turn the page.

Go for it.

# Chapter 1

# MARRIAGE:
# THE BEST SEXUAL POSITION

**Man**
*Oh, if I could build my whole world
around you
I'd give you the greatest gift any woman
could possess*

**Woman**
*And I'd step into this world you've created
And give you true love and tenderness*
**– Marvin Gaye and Tammie Terrell**

*Whisper to me softly while the moon is low
Hold me close and tell me what I want to
know
Say it to me gently, let the sweet talk flow
Come a little closer . . . make love to me*
**– Jo Stafford**

When you get married, is there any good sex after the honeymoon?

You bet.

After the first year?

Yup.

*Great* sex?

Yes.

Frequent?

Yes.

After five, ten, twenty, thirty, and forty years?

Absolutely.

Fifty and sixty?

I'll let you know.

Just don't believe all the comments out there in our culture that say that marriage makes the sex go bad. Those comments are said by people in bad or mediocre marriages having bad or mediocre sex, and they say it so often that other people believe them and start to say it too, and then everybody believes it.

But none of it's true.

The *opposite* is true.

Marriage is a wonderful place for sex. Marriage is where sex and love melt into each other and become one. Marriage *perfects* sex.

After an evening of good marital sex, you and your wife are lying next to each other in bed holding hands, silent in the dim light, slightly dazed and sweetly tired, and one of you gently interrupts the silence and says, "I can't believe we're *married* and have an actual *license* to do this."

If you want that in your marriage, you can have it. There are a few steps involved, but you can have it.

Here's the first step:

Go to your wife and ask her what she thinks needs to happen in your marriage for the two of you to have better and more frequent sex. Ask her what she thinks needs to happen for you to have *spectacular* sex.

*"Talk to me more,"* she might say.

*"Share your thoughts and feelings with me more. Let me*

*know what's going on inside you."*

*"Be nicer to me."*

*"Learn how to be affectionate with me without trying to make it sexual."*

*"Don't be so busy all the time."*

*"Don't smell like beer all the time."*

*"Lose some weight. Look sexier to me."*

*"Ask me what I like in sex. Ask me about my sexuality."*

*"Stop looking at other women."*

*"Desist, delete, destroy, and throw all pornography out of your life."*

*"Dedicate your life to learning how to be a good husband to me."*

Totally believe her, and start to do everything she wants you to do.

# Chapter 2

# THE VARIETIES OF MARITAL SEX: THE BAD, THE GOOD, AND THE SNUGGLY

> *There's nothing better than good sex. But bad sex? A peanut butter and jelly sandwich is better than bad sex.*
> **– Billy Joel**

> *Marriage is honorable in all, and the bed undefiled.*
> **– Hebrews 13:4**

Bad sex takes many forms in marriage. It's too depressing to write about them all, but here's one:

Bad sex in marriage is when a sexually aroused man starts fiddling and diddling with the sexual parts of his wife's body until she gets turned on enough that maybe she'll start fiddling and diddling with his sexual part until he gets to put his sexual part inside her sexual part and ejaculate. Bad sex in marriage is when a so-called adult man is touching his wife like a rabid fourteen-year-old boy with a boner. And bad sex in marriage is when his wife, somehow pretending to enjoy any of that, calls it sex.

Because it's not sex.

And it's not sexy.

It's a drag. Hardly worth it. No wonder so many wives don't care about it anymore.

Good sex in marriage is something completely different. Good marital sex is when a husband actually *knows* his wife sexually – knows her sexual body *(I want a man with a slow hand)*, knows her sexual desires *(I want a lover with an easy touch)*, and sexual fantasies *(I want somebody who will spend some time)*, and sexual needs *(not come and go in a heated rush)*, and he knows how to really make love to her, and she knows how to really make love to him, and both of them get into bed often and make really sweet love to each other. Good marital sex is when two people who know each other and love each other enter a private palace of pleasure and happiness for a while, sometimes a long while, exploring its many rooms and recesses and hallways and chambers, saying and doing some very interesting things to each other, and then they emerge some time later, tired, relaxed, in love, and hungry.

Good sex in marriage can be two ways, one way, and each and every way the two of you have the imagination and the energy and the time for. It can be sliding and gliding around in bed together with wild desire, or it can be snuggling on the couch together in your pajamas with your little bowls of ice cream in your laps, watching reruns of *Colombo*. Good sex in marriage can be strong and hard and quick, like a sudden storm, a *collision* of hands and mouths and bodies and sound; or it can be slow and delicate and soft, as soft and slight as what you whisper to each other as you fall asleep together, your hand on her soft thigh under the blankets, at midnight. It can be loud or silent, a squeeze of her arm as you walk by her in the doorway, a look in her eyes as she sees you coming up the stairs with your shirt open. Good sex in marriage is everything you do with each other, everything you say to each other, every way you touch each other, every time you get near each other. Good sex in marriage sometimes leads to orgasm, sometimes not, but it always leads to more closeness and love.

If, as they say, variety is the spice of life, good sex in marriage is very spicy because there are so many varieties of it. There are so many kinds and types of marital sex and so many occasions and reasons for it. Here are a few of them:

There's the *Can-You-Come-Over-Here-And-Help-Me-Out-For-A-Second?*...the *Let's-Jump-Into-Bed-For-A-Quickie*...the *Morning-Wake-Up*...the *After-The-Big-Fight-Make-Up*...the *Let's-Lie-Down-For-Our-Lunch-Break*...the *Afternoon-Delight*...the *Good-Fun-Day-Together-Nightcap*...the *Serious-Sex-After-A-Serious-Talk*...*the Clothes-Flying-Off-I've-Got-To-Have-You-RIGHT-NOW!*...the *Do-We-Really-Think-That-Nobody-Was-Watching-When-We-Did-It-Inside-A-Large-Shrub-In-A-Small-Public-Park-In-Lincoln-Nebraska-On-Our-Cross-Country-Trip-In-1975?*...the *Winter-Evening-On-The-Livingroom-Rug-By-The-Fire*...the *All-Nighter* (expires after having children or attaining the age of 37)...the *Full-Body-Massage-With-Oil-To-The-Sounds-Of-Birds-Chirping-In-The-Brazilian-Rainforest*...the...*I-Think-We-Just-Went-To-Heaven-And-Saw-God*...the *We're-On-Vacation-In-A-Fancy-Hotel-Room-With-A-Bottle-Of-Wine-Extravaganza*...the *We're-On-The-Phone-Saying-VERY-Sexy-Things-To-Each-Other-And-Breathing-Fast!*...the *I'm-*

*Too-Tired-Old-Depressed-And-Upset-To-Do-Anything-But-Lie-Here-And-Groan-While-You-Do-Everything-Else-Please...the Don't-You-Dare-Tell-Anybody-I'm-Into-THIS!...*the *After-Sex-Next-Morning-Sweet-Little-Post-Toastie...*and whatever other names, brands, occasions, times, places, reasons, opportunities, or excuses for sex you and your wife can cook up between you. Enjoy them all. Some are short, some are long, most are legal, some are unbelievable, but they're all enjoyable. *"Gonna find my baby, gonna hold her tight, gonna grab some afternoon delight. "* They're all delightful varieties of great sex. They're all marriage.

And because they're all marriage, they're all good. Remember: *Marriage is honorable in all, and the bed undefiled.* The couch is also undefiled, and so is the car, and the livingroom rug in front of the fireplace, and the kitchen counter, and the shower, and the large shrub in the small public park in Lincoln, Nebraska in 1975.

# Chapter 3

## THE GROUND RULES FOR A TRULY SEXUAL MARRIAGE

> When the one man loves the one woman
> and the one woman loves the one man,
> the very angels desert heaven and come and
> sit in that house and sing for joy
> **– Brahma Sutras**

> You're the queen of my flesh, girl,
> You're my woman, you're my delight
> You're the lamp of my soul, girl,
> And you torch up the night
> **– Bob Dylan**

When a man loves a woman, he wants to *make* love to that woman – all his life, if he's lucky enough to marry her. To him her body is a garden of earthly delights, a kind of heaven on earth, a wonderland, and when he makes love to her, he enters a realm of such unbelievable pleasure and love and enjoyment that it's hard for us men to put it into words, so for lack of a better word we just call it sex.

The word that comes closest to describing sex for us men is *fun*. Sex is *a lot* of fun for us. It's the kind of fun we had as boys playing on our football fields and basketball courts and frozen ponds and playgrounds, but better because this time the playground has a vagina! It's the kind of fun that most of us don't have in the

9

jobs we have to go to every day – we're not boys playing games anymore, we're men working jobs to provide for our families – so we like looking forward to having fun with our wives when we get the chance.

You'd think that if something was that much fun and therefore that important to a married man, he'd know more about it. Or learn more about it. Or figure out the different things he had to do and say to his wife to get more of it. You'd think.

I shudder to think what I didn't know about sex when I was a young married man in the 1970s and 80s. Nobody had ever taught me anything useful about sex except the girl I first had sex with in 1963 as a freshman at Cornell, the girl from Cortland College with the gold front tooth, who, while I was trying manfully to have intercourse with her one very drunk night at a fraternity party, whispered in my ear, very kindly, "Not there," after which I passed out. The other two places I had gotten any sexual information from were *Playboy* magazine and my best friend Kenny Schwartz, both of whom were very big on breasts.

That was it. The rest of it was me and my wife just figuring it out together as we went along. Every married couple has to stumble and bumble their way through sex together, no matter what their sexual experience or expertise coming into the marriage, but if the two people really love each other and want to really get to know each other, they can get through the stumbles and bumbles, and their sex becomes a really nice thing they learn how to do together over many years.

I could have saved myself one or two stumbles and 1,282,657

bumbles if, when I was a young married man, I had known more about sex and about marriage and about womanhood and about my wife. I wish someone had shown up to tell me the kind of man I would have to be and the things I would have to do and say as a husband, in and out of the bedroom, to be a really good lover to her. I had to figure it all out by myself, which was okay, because I did, mostly, but I wish someone who had some knowledge of how to be a great husband and lover had passed it down to me earlier.

So to that young man in 1974, three years married, living with his young wife and young daughter in the beautiful Berkshire Mountains of western Massachusetts, to that young man who thought his wife was the most beautiful woman he had ever seen, surpassing Betty *and* Veronica – in fact, she *was* Betty, with Veronica *inside!* – this is what I would say to him, this is what I would tell him about how to have a lot of sexual fun with his wife for the rest of his life:

## How Do I Love Thee? Let Me Count the Ways

Love her. Just love her. The way to love her is to love her in all the ways she likes to be loved. How can you know all the ways she likes to be loved? Numbskull, she's been trying to tell you the ways she likes to be loved from the moment she first met you, so just *listen* to her. If she likes to be loved by you telling her she's beautiful every day, tell her she's beautiful every day. If she likes to be loved by you taking walks with her, take walks with her. And *talk* with her! – she's already told you about a trillion times she likes it when you talk with her, so talk with her. If she likes to be loved by you not leaving your dirty dishes in the sink or your socks on the floor, don't leave your dirty dishes in the sink or your socks on the floor. If she likes to be loved by you not flirting with other women anymore, don't flirt with other women anymore, don't even *look* at other women, she doesn't like that. If she likes to be loved by you opening car doors for her, open car doors for her. If she likes to be loved by you *not* opening car doors for her, don't open car doors for her. (See how simple this is?) If she likes to be loved by you not raising your voice to her anymore and always being gentle and sweet and kind and caring to her, stop getting so irritated with her and angry at her and just be gentle and sweet and kind and caring to her. It is your job as her husband to love her in these ways, so be a man and do your job. Count all the ways you love her, and keep adding to your count. That's your job. If you do a good job, you will be very well-compensated, with great benefits and big bonuses.

Loving your wife in all the ways she likes to be loved is your best shot at getting a lot of good sex in your marriage because the way a woman's love works is that when she's given love by you, she wants to give love back to you, including giving you her sexual love. Women are great *givers* – they *give* birth, they *give* milk, they *give* their hands in marriage, they *give* their hearts away, and they *give* sex; but the thing to know about women is that they're givers-*back* – they give when they're given to. It is amazing sex when a married woman is giving her sexual love to a husband she wants to give back to. And it will be amazing sex given to you – when you give your wife amazing love.

*******

## Le Chevalier Sans Reproche

You don't have to invent this kind of love. It's already in you. It's in all men. It's the knight, the one in shining armor on a horse, the noble knight, the *chevalier sans reproche.* The knightly tradition of chivalry lives in you as the best part of your manhood. The knight in you is courteous, strong, wise, humble, and respectful. He is good-natured, generous, magnanimous, and helpful. His deepest desire in life is to serve – faithful service is his highest value – and he is totally loyal to those he serves. He has integrity – he says what he means and does what he says; you can trust him. He is on a constant quest to improve himself. He is manly and tough and brave and not afraid of hardships and not afraid of a fight. He is the *chevalier sans peur.* He wants to win honor, and he wants to win the admiration and love of the lady whom he loves and honors. His overwhelming, passionate, devotional love for his lady is, for him, the source of all endeavor and excellence. His love for her is a religion to him, imposing on him disciplines of mind and body and behavior, and giving him a high and noble purpose in life, which is to win her and serve her.

If you want to see an actual man who is a modern version of this knight, read about Felipe, the *Br*azilian man who appears in Elizabeth Gilbert's life in Bali in the "Love" chapter of her international bestseller ***Eat, Pray, Love.*** She describes Felipe: *"He's a caregiver by nature, and I can feel him going into a kind of orbit around me, making me the key directional setting for his compass, growing into the role of being my attendant knight. . . . He is organizing himself around me. It's lovely to be treated this way."*

Felipe consecrates himself to the care of Elizabeth. Lying in bed next to him while he sleeps, Elizabeth contemplates Felipe: *"I'm not sure what I want. I do know that there's a part of me which has always wanted to hear a man say, 'Let me take care of you forever,' and I have never heard it spoken before. Over the last few years, I'd given up looking for that person, learned how to say this heartening sentence to myself, especially in times of fear. But to hear it from someone else now, from someone who is speaking sincerely . . ."* Then, getting tired, she stops thinking about it and just holds him, thinking one last thought before she slips into sleep: *"I am falling in love with this man . . ."*

Take a wild guess why this woman falls in love with Felipe.

Take another wild guess why a gazillion women around the globe bought the book.

*Deus abençoi o Brasil!*

The lady falls in love with the *chevalier sans reproche.* Your lady will too – because he is who you really are. The way the knight feels about his lady is how you really feel about your wife. That's why you married her – to take care of her forever. Lady Elizabeth. Lady Lucia. Lady Lyubochka. Lady Michelle. Lady Zulaikha. Lady Mizuki. Lady Elena. Lady Cécile. Lady Hantaywee. Lady Lakshmi. Lady Dina. Lady Ying. Lady Jazlyne. Lady Giuliana. Lady Jane. Pledge yourself to Lady Jane. When you do, when you pledge your troth and your honor and your service to your lady, like the knights of old you win her love, and then she will allow you, like the knights of old, into her chamber.

*******

## Semper Fidelis

Never be unfaithful to your wife. Now that you're married, for the rest of your life never touch sexually any woman but her. It is not okay, and it is never okay. There are no explanations, rationalizations, justifications, victimizations, exceptions, self-deceptions, excuses, exemptions, or alibis that make it okay.

Never be unfaithful to your wife. If you're unfaithful to her, I guarantee you, it will last forever as an unhealable wound in her heart. A husband's infidelity is like a dagger to a woman's heart. She takes the dagger with her to her grave. A husband's infidelity is the desolate face of the politician's wife as she stands on the podium behind him as he makes his public confession of adultery. It's that sadness, that blank bereavement in her eyes, that bombed-out stare. She takes that with her to her grave too. You want to see *that* in your wife's face?

Never be unfaithful to your wife. It's *really* stupid. If you want to have a lot of good marital sex with your wife for the rest of your life, extramarital sex is the *worst* thing you could do. You're trying to get her to like you and respect you and adore you and totally love you so she'll want to give herself in sex to you, but, schmuck, your extramarital sex will make her *hate* you, distrust you, turn away from you, close down to you. The absolute *un*sexiest thing you could ever do to your wife is to have sex with another woman.

Never be unfaithful to your wife. Being a man, your sexual wanting runs wild in your mind sometimes, but keep it there, in your mind, and bring all that sex and all that wanting and all that mind to the marriage with your wife. Not until she feels all your sexuality coming only to her, not until it's pointed exclusively to her, can she take all of it into her.

Never be unfaithful to your wife. Contain your sexuality completely within your marriage. The true flower of marital sexuality grows only in an *enclosed* garden, the *hortus conclusus* of marriage. *"Let my beloved come into his garden, and eat his pleasant fruits."* Your faithfulness to her is the only gate that opens into that garden, to eat those fruits.

*******

## Beyond Pornography

Don't succumb to pornography. That won't be easy because wherever you go in your life, pornography will be there. It's all over the place. It'll be on the cover of *Life* magazine in 1954 where a little eight-year-old boy named Bobby saw Marilyn Monroe and touched her glossy cleavage; and it'll be on a million other magazine covers, and billboards, and television shows, and movies, and commercials, and computers, hard porn, soft porn, the hypnotic power of a woman's sexual body over your poor defenseless eyes. It's everywhere, and it's out to get you.

So don't let it. Don't succumb. Be stronger than it. Remember that the inevitable outcome of all pornography is addiction to sex or boredom with sex, usually both. Don't let them do that to sex for you, young man. If they've already done it, if you already have a weakness for pornography, remember that it's a *weakness*, and weakness does not become a man. Don't be a weak man, be a strong man. A strong man gives his strong sexuality to his wife instead of dribbling it away at the computer. If you have pornographic fantasies floating around in your head, bring as many of them into the sex with your wife as she'll allow (she may have her own too, by the way), and leave the other fantasies behind along with all your other pornographic paraphernalia. Now that you're a married man, you're a mature man with a mature man's sexuality. You've outgrown pornography. Pornography is childish sexuality. Now that you've become a man, it's time to put away your childish things.

*******

### Getting a Little Nookie Tonight?

Believe it or not, your wife does not get sexually turned on when you talk about sex like a giggling, sniggling adolescent boy. As hard as it may be, at least *pretend* to be an adult man when you talk about sex with her or ask her for it. Making love to your wife is *not* "hiding the salami" or "getting a little nookie tonight" or "stirring the macaroni" or "downloading your software" or "the horizontal hokey-pokey." And her breasts aren't a rack, or boobs, bombs, knobs, knockers, honkers, highbeams, balloons, jugs, tits, tatas, torpedoes, winnebagoes, whoppers, melons, cupcakes, casabas, gazongas, or hooters, they're *breasts,* her beautiful, beautiful breasts, and they don't exist so you can be pawing at them every single time you see them.

It is fine to keep all your youthful wonderment and enthusiasm for sex, young man, and it is fine for you to be so adolescent about it and so uncomfortable with it that all you can do is make stupid dumbass jokes and sleazy little puns about it – she's okay with that sometimes, she already knows how dreadfully immature you are

– but you can't be that juvenile about sex *all* the time – she hates that – so sometimes you have to do something that most of us men find it hard to do about sex, which is to grow up.

*******

## Sacred Space

Respect your wife's physical and sexual boundaries, young man. Yes, she's beautiful, yes, she's touchable, yes, she's sexual, but remember, she's not always *available.* There'll be times when you'll go to her and you'll say or do something sexual to her and she'll let you know – either by telling you directly or by some subtle, indirect signal like sawing your hands off with her nail file – that she's not interested in sex right now. She may actually come out and say, *"I'm not interested in sex right now;"* or she may say, *"That's not where I'm at right now"* . . . *"I'm in the middle of doing something"* . . . *"I'm enjoying just lying here reading my magazine"* . . . *"I'm too tired"* . . . *"I'm too mad at you"* . . . *"I'm not in the mood right now"* . . . *"Not tonight, dear, I have to get up early tomorrow morning"* . . . *"Not tonight, dear, I have a concussion."* These words do not mean that there's anything wrong with you, your sexual technique, your marriage, her libido, or her – they just mean she doesn't want to have sex with you right now. They mean that she's an actual person whose sole purpose on this earth is not to be always sexually available to you. They mean she's a woman, guardian of the sacred space of vagina and womb, herself sacred space – and she doesn't want you in it right now; and though you might feel like getting angry, cranky, sulky, sullen, surly, pouty, petulant, depressed, and psychotic in reaction to that, you're not supposed to *show* that reaction to her. Keep it inside. Show her some maturity. Show her some respect. Whenever you approach her space wanting to enter it, approach respectfully, and whenever she doesn't want you in it, back away gracefully.

*******

## Sex Without End

As pleasures go on this earth, orgasm is one of the best – for both men and women – and if it's a regular part of your marital sexuality, great! – knock yourselves out, have a million of them. There's only one problem with orgasm in marital sexuality – it tends to *end* the sexuality, either suddenly and right away or more gradually but soon. It gives sex a direction to go in, a destination to get to, and therefore a limit. As limits go, orgasm's a blast, but it's still a limit, and sometimes you and your wife might experience orgasms as a *limitation*, an inner pressure to have one, like an obligation, and if you don't have one, a disappointment or a personal failure. Sex that's *always* headed toward orgasm is going to get less sexy over time. So some of the time you and your wife might want to explore having sex with no orgasms at the end, which will take self-restraint, but it might be worth it. You might find yourselves having sex that lasts longer, with more novelty and variety, more excitement, more love, more fun, and *more sex* than you were having when you were having orgasms. Try it sometimes – you and your wife might like it – sex that has no direction, no goal, no orgasm at the end of it, and therefore no end of it, but just the two of you sexually circling and circling around each other on the marriage bed, delight without destination, sex without end, amen.

*******

## Remember Zorba

Remember that you have had the great good fortune to meet and marry a woman who you find beautiful and sexual and who has put herself in the sexual care of you. You have been given one of the greatest treasures a man can have on this earth – a lovely wife who loves you – and now you're responsible for her – including *sexually* responsible for her – for the rest of your life. That means you must do whatever you have to do, adopt any discipline, read any book, go to any therapist, do everything you can to bring the sexual man that you are to the sexual woman you were lucky enough to marry. If that means learning how to talk to your wife, stopping ogling other women, keeping yourself in shape so you look sexy to her, you do all that. You get to the man she wants you to get to so you can get to her. You are her partner, her lover, the prince consort of her desire, and when she desires you to come in unto her, you're supposed to go. You've got to bring it – to *her.* *"God has a very big heart,"* says Zorba the Greek, *"but there is one sin He will not forgive – if a woman calls a man to her bed, and he will not go."*

# Chapter 4

# THE HEALING POWER
# OF MARITAL SEX

*Sex is difficult; yes.*
**– Rainer Marie Rilke**

*When the energies of romantic passion are
contained and stabilized by commitment
and discipline, marriage becomes an emotional bond and a transformative process
equal to any other structure for personal
growth yet devised by human beings.*
**– Harville Hendrix**

As a psychotherapist and marriage counselor for the past thirty-six years, one of my jobs has been to help married couples
create the kind of marriage from which arises the kind of marital
sex I'm talking about in this book. The first thing I have to do is to
tell the couple that that kind of sex is not only possible in marriage
but natural to it, and one of the main reasons they don't have that
yet is the sexual damage that was done to all of us collectively and
to each of us individually before we ever got into our marriages.
Sexually speaking, we're all damaged because we've all grown up
in a sexually damaged global culture, and we bring every bit of that
damage into our marriages.

The other reason why consistently great sex is difficult to

achieve in marriage is because sex – because it's *sex*, the most open, private, secret, uninhibited thing you can do with another human being, involving aspects of your energy and parts of your body that are *so* private and vulnerable and mind-blowingly, heart-stoppingly pleasurable that it's a wonder any of us can muster up enough courage and maturity to do it at all – great marital sex is a tricky business. Trying to get to *that* kind of sex between two married human beings is, as we used to say in the sixties, *a trip* – and trips can take a while and be difficult.

That's why most married couples who have come to see me for therapy in the past thirty-six years have had sexual problems. Usually the husband thinks there's something wrong with his wife's sexuality, and the wife thinks there's something wrong with her husband's sexuality. Usually they're both right, but it doesn't really matter – we have to fix it all anyway.

*"We haven't had sex in a month,"* couples say.

*"We haven't had sex in three months,"* they say.

*"We haven't had sex in a year,"* they say.

*"Our sex is so mechanical and dull, it's hardly worth it,"* they say.

*"What's wrong with us?"* they say.

*"More than you probably want to know,"* I say.

But I tell them anyway.

What's wrong with us is that every one of us is a piece of sexual wreckage. Each one of us, by virtue of having been born into this world and then carried across the stormy sea of its sexuality for so many years, is sexually wrecked. Men are wrecked in one way, and women in another, and we're all individually and uniquely wrecked – *custom*-wrecked – by our personal life experience and sexual history. Some of us are oversexed, addicted to sex, addicted to pornography, masturbation, and all manner of inappropriate and inadvisable sex, some of which is unconscionable and criminal. Some of us are undersexed, turned off by sex, fearful or ashamed or repulsed by sex, judging and maligning sex, numb to sex. And some of us are just weirdly sexed, which we hide pretty well from everybody except when we get near ladies wearing flame-red lipstick or very attractive poultry. We're all victims and only partial survivors of a tumultuous sexual sea littered with the sexual wreckage of all the human generations before us. Trying to stay sexually afloat in the pummeling of those waters has made most of us pretty deranged about sex. I have never met anyone who wasn't, in one way or another, pretty deranged about sex. I have never met anyone who made it across that sea unwrecked.

What happens when two sexually wrecked beings accidentally bump into each other on a random wave in that sea? They start swimming together for awhile, and the sex between them is new and sexy and frequent and fun, and some of those people decide to *stay* swimming together and wash up on the shore of marriage together. They try their best to make the sex continue to work in their marriage, and sometimes it does, even very well, for a while, but in millions of marriages after a while it doesn't work so well, and stops being sexy and stops being frequent and stops being fun, and for some married couples it just stops, period. There's a lot of pain on the way to its stopping, and there is more pain, a deeper, lonelier pain, after it stops. If the wife and husband in the marriage are lazy, they'll let the sexual pain go on for so long that they'll settle dejectedly into a dreary sex life or none at all; or they'll bring their sexuality outside the marriage into extramarital sex (or into pornography, which is a kind of extramarital sex), which wreaks havoc in the marriage, the children, the society, and the whole universe; or they'll end the marriage after a few years and seek better sex with somebody else. That's if they're lazy. If the wife and husband aren't lazy and have some gumption, they'll seek help – from therapists, friends, books, online, wherever they can find it – and get some advice on how to solve their sexual problems.

Here's some advice:

To solve your sexual problems and start enjoying lifelong sexual fun with your spouse, the first thing that each of you must do is admit that you're both pieces of sexual wreckage. No big deal; remember – we're all pawns in this game, we are all sexually damaged. The next thing to do is to learn everything you can about the particular sexual damage done to you and the particular sexual damage done to your spouse and bring that all to light by talking about it with each other. Sometimes you may need the help of a counselor to talk about it, which is fine as long as you're talking about it. By talking about it, you start understanding it, and by understanding it, you gain control over it and develop the power to change it – to repair the sexual wreckage that the two of you are. Remember that one of God's intentions for marriage is for repair of all forms of human wreckage, and that includes sexual wreckage. These things can get healed in marriage.

So when the two of you close the bedroom door and slip into bed for sex, stay in more than physical touch with each other, stay in emotional touch, and from time to time be talking about what's going on for each of you during sex.

*How does that feel? . . . Do you like to be touched here? . . . Here? . . . Uh, what's that over there? . . . What are you experiencing right now? . . . What are you feeling? . . . Are you distracted, or nervous, or feeling shy right now? . . . Are you having a bad memory? . . . Should we stop for a while? . . . I'd like to stop for a while. . . . I'd like you to do this now, but gently, and very, very slowly. . . . Is this okay? . . . Could you say something sexy? . . . In Yiddish? . . . Could you touch me there? . . . That's good, keep going. . . . Is it okay to say the words that are in my mind right now? . . . Can I share a fantasy with you right now? . . . Uh, now? . . . I just got scared for a second. I think I need to take a break. . . . When I close my eyes, I keep seeing my uncle. . . . Hold me now, just hold me. . . . Tell me you love me. . . . Can we rest now? . . . Let's just lie here and rest now . . .*

And so, having reached the shore of marriage together, that beautiful beach, two sexual wrecks use the sexual energy between them to repair their wreckage. Over the course of their marriage, gradually, patiently, lovingly, they heal their sexuality. It can take a long time. That's okay, marriage *is* a long time, and what better way to spend a long time than having sex on a beach with your sweetheart.

# Chapter 5

# THE GAUNTLET:
# YOUR WIFE'S SEXUAL HISTORY

> Girls and women who are sexually
> violated experience the most extreme
> form of a process that occurs for all
> women.
> **– Jean Baker Miller**

> My love, she's like some raven
> at my window with a broken wing
> **– Bob Dylan**

In all your sexual behaviors with your wife, treat her with great respect. Respect what she wants and doesn't want. Do what she likes and don't do what she doesn't like. In your marriage, in your sexual treatment of your wife, restore the respect for woman and for woman's sexuality that has been so absent in your wife's experience. By word or deed never dishonor, demean, defile, or abuse her sexuality. She's already had enough of that. She's *already* been sexually defiled and abused. All of world culture is a long gauntlet of sexual abuse that every girl and woman runs from birth to death. Sexual abuse is just what *happens* to women in this world, including to your wife.

Here's the way I see it:

Any woman who has ever been stared at, leered at, eyed, ogled, or looked up and down for the purpose of sexual appraisal by a man has been sexually abused. Any woman who has ever had her blouse stared down or her skirt stared up has been sexually abused. Any woman who has ever seen a movie, television show, computer, commercial, billboard, or magazine in which a sexually suggestive woman was displayed has been sexually abused. Any woman who has ever been sexually spoken to, joked about, or propositioned by a man who feels he has the right to do that simply because she's a woman has been sexually abused. Any woman who has ever been forced to see any gesture of disrespectful and aggressive male sexuality has been sexually abused. Any woman who has ever heard an aggressive whistle, lewd comment, or angry obscenity from a man has been sexually abused. Any woman who has ever been invited into, or exposed to, male pornography has been sexually abused. Any woman who has ever been touched, pinched, patted, petted, rubbed, groped, stroked, hugged, or kissed without her invitation or against her will has been sexually abused. Any woman who has ever said no to a man's sexual advances and the man didn't immediately stop his sexual advances has been sexually abused. Any woman who's ever been stalked has been sexually abused. Any woman who has ever been made to feel that her job, her financial security, her physical safety, her marriage, her womanhood, or her human worth was a function of the way she looked or dressed or sexually performed has been sexually abused. Any woman who has ever been misled, deceived, or emotionally manipulated by a male for his sexual purposes has been sexually abused. Any woman who has ever been overpowered by a man's command or demand or ultimatum or threat to have sex with him has been sexually abused. Any woman who has ever been physically forced to perform any sexual act with a man – raped – has been sexually abused

All of these are violations of a woman's psychological, physical, and sexual boundaries. They all put the woman on notice that she is being seen, talked about, thought of, and treated as a sexual body that could be approached, possessed, used, and abused for the sexual pleasure of a male.

It happens to all women in our culture.

And a lot worse.

What happened to your wife?

Do you know?

You should want to know.

Ask her about it.

What's the gauntlet been like for her? What's her story?

She's got a story. She's got a history. If you show real interest, perhaps she'll tell it to you.

And when she does, when she tells you about the stranger in the elevator, or her cousin in the attic that time, or her uncle all those years, or her counselor, or neighbor, or her high school boyfriend in the car that night at the golf course, or her first husband when he'd be drunk, when she tells you about the looks, the comments, the passes and promises, the lies, all the *hands,* and the tremendous pressure that's been brought to bear on her, when she tells you, listen.

And if she cries, hold her and listen.

And if she gets angry, let her get angry, and hold her and listen.

And when she's done and sitting there silent and distant in her eyes, just sit there with her and tell her you understand the sexual wounds she's suffered and the scars she bears – the sexual disrespect and desecration of her womanhood that she's borne – and you're so glad she's made it to the end of the gauntlet – made it to *you* – because you're going to be the *opposite* of all that – you're going to be a man who respects her sexuality – and change history.

# Chapter 6

# BECOMING A BETTER LOVER

*Why don't you tell me, lovin' mama, how
you want your rollin' done?
Why don't you tell me, lovin' mama,
how you want your rollin' done?
Lord, I give you satisfaction now if it's all
night long . . .*
**– Big Bill Broonzy**

I hate to be the one to have to tell you this, but I think a lot of us guys are not great lovers to our wives. We've spent thousands of years blaming the women for the absence or infrequency of good sex in our marriages – *"You're never interested in sex anymore."* . . . *"You never want it anymore."* . . . *"You're never in the mood anymore."* . . . *"You never reach orgasm anymore."* . . . *"You seem so cold, like you don't get turned on anymore."* – but maybe that's all bullshit, maybe it's us guys who have *caused* that, maybe we're just not good lovers to them.

Here's a way to become a good lover to your wife:

Assume that when it comes to your wife's sexuality – which is *female* sexuality – you know basically nothing. That means that for the rest of your life you are a *student* of your wife's female sexuality. Female sexuality is different than male sexuality, so you have to learn it. There are different sexual body parts to learn about, different hormones, the lunar cycle, the life cycle, female sexual conditioning, your wife's personal sexual psychology, and whatever sexual quirks and curiosities she's bringing into the marriage from God knows (and you're probably better off *not* knowing) where she picked them up. That's a lot of learning, which is why we men need to be lifetime students of our wife's sexuality.

And they should be lifetime students of ours.

Which means that marriage is a long course of sex education for both husband and wife, a whole curriculum, and we married people should be doing a lot of studying which, in the case of marital sex, means a lot of thinking about and talking about sex with your spouse. (If you want, you can think of it as boning up on the subject. You might even pull a few all-nighters.) We should be doing a lot of asking and a lot of answering about sex – explaining and describing our respective sexualites to each other, teaching each other how to touch us and hold us and kiss us and excite us and drive us out of our minds with pleasure when they make love to us.

It's hard to talk about sex, though, even for married couples, because it's such a sensitive subject, as sensitive and delicate as the sexual parts of us that we're talking about. It's hard to tell somebody you love how to do something right without telling them that they're doing it wrong. It's hard to overcome a natural shyness most of us have about sex and talk about how it really works for us. It's hard to say to someone, "What you're doing right there is making me feel a little seasick, but if you do it right *here* you'll make me come." It's hard to say that kind of stuff.

But say it anyway. Teach each other sex. Have and keep having the sexual conversation as you have and keep having sex.

Make the sexual conversation an ongoing conversation that goes on for the whole length of your marriage. In bed and out of bed, you and your wife tell each other how you're wired-up sexually: what you like and what you don't like; what turns you on and what doesn't; which side of your neck, when kissed, is titillating, and which side just tickles; how it feels when you're touched there, or there, or there; what tiredness does to your sexual feelings, or anger, or marital discord, or a bad week at work; how your sexual feelings are changing as you mature and have babies and your bodies get older. Tell each other. Show and tell. In bed and out of bed, keep talking about it, keep teaching it to each other. Sex is a graduate course you both signed up for when you signed up for marriage. Marriage is the highest degree you can get in sex.

When you're sitting in your wife's classroom and she's teaching you about how sex works for her, listen. If her talking about her sexuality gives you an erection, listen *up*. Remember that male sexuality has been center stage on the planet for the last ten thousand years, and female sexuality – strong, beautiful, colossal female sexuality – has been offstage and is coming onstage now – center stage – everywhere in the world, including in your marriage. Listen to what your wife is trying to tell you about her sexuality. Listen to her personal vagina monologue. Pay attention, ask questions, take notes, come to class. Your wife's sexuality is the subject of the course, and your wife is the teacher. Respect your teacher highly, and learn your subject well. Become a great lover to her.

Do you think a great lover, someone who *really* knows how to make love to his wife, is going to get more and better sex with her? You think you want to come to this school? You think this is a class worth taking? You think this is a curriculum worth following? Can you *imagine* the homework?

# Chapter 7

# UNDERSTANDING FEMALE SEXUALITY: EVERYTHING IS FOREPLAY

*Our love is kind of stalled, baby*
*But it ain't about the sex*
*I'd trade the roses and the negligees*
*If we could just connect*
**– Bonnie Raitt**

Your wife's sexuality is one of the greatest gifts that will ever be given to you on this earth. You know that. She's given it. And it blew your mind.

To make sure her sexuality is a gift that keeps on giving, make sure you *understand* her sexuality.

It's *female* sexuality.

Which, in case you hadn't noticed, is not exactly the same as male sexuality.

Male sexuality, as I see it, is basically a man somewhat clumsily fumbling and bumbling with the sexual parts of a woman until she, against all odds, gets fired up enough to pay attention to *his* sexual part, which has been hard and throbbing and actually *steaming* for hours, so he can finally have his orgasm and relax. There are more sophisticated versions of this that can involve expensive restaurants and fine wines and tall candles and the Mantovani strings, but it's basically the same thing.

You husbands who are good lovers to your wives – and you husbands who aren't such good lovers yet but are at least *trying* – more power to you, because you empower and ennoble your wife's female sexuality; but remember – up to this point in history, most of female sexuality has been a woman's attempt to fit her own vast sexuality onto the sorry little thing her man happens to be offering up to her, and then using all her willpower to keep from yawning, crying, laughing, or reading during it.

Now let's talk about how female sexuality actually works.

First off, to get it, you can't just show up at her body with a blazing hard-on at some random moment of the week and say, "Here am I!"

Most of the time it doesn't quite work like that for her.

The way her sexuality works is that it starts much earlier than you think it does. It's a long ramp that starts way back with how you've actually been *relating* to her, *treating* her, all the rest of the week.

Imagine that.

Are you attentive to her? Are you nice to her? Do you talk with her about her life? Are you interested in her feelings about things? Do you know she *has* feelings? Do you know how she likes to be touched? Are you interested? Do you ask her? Do you express your appreciation and admiration of her – her good heart, her intelligence and wisdom, her competence, her constancy, her beautiful face and body? All your positive feelings toward her and the ways that you express them – your hug in the morning, your phone call and your text in the afternoon and your pleasant conversation at dinner, your thoughtfulness and kindness and gentleness and sweetness, your interest in her and your attentiveness to her, all that warmth you give her during the day is what gets her hot at night.

The trick is to stay *connected* to her, because female sexuality is completely connected to how connected she feels to you.

Got that?

Just in case you missed it, I'll repeat it:

*Female sexuality is completely connected to how connected she feels to you.*

Imagine *that.*

All that time you spend out of bed with her, the thousand and one little connections you create with her, are *erotic* to her! All the ways that you show love and respect to your wife are – in that slow, softening, melting, liquefying way of a woman – turning her on!

The ancient Greek poetess Sappho said it long ago:

> *How love*
> *the limb-loosener*
> *sweeps me away!*

That's it! – for a woman, the limb-loosener is *love!*

A good husband is a great lover.

He is making love to his wife basically *all the time.*

So, if you want the gift of your wife's sexuality, give her the gift she wants from you. Start to be nice as pie to her. Sweet as honey. Considerate. Interested. Supportive. Helpful. Kind. Give her your time and your attention. Your appreciation and your gratitude. Go be with her, and be good to her. Be *nice* to her.

In the way you talk with her, in the way you are with her, always show your love and respect for her. In the little things you do and in the big things you do, create connection with her.

It's all foreplay, man.

# Chapter 8

# CONNECTING WITH YOUR WIFE'S SEXUALITY: FOLLOWING HER CURVES

*The nakedness of woman is the work of God.*
**– William Blake**

*They all want me to rock them*
*like my back ain't got no bone*
*I want a man to rock me*
*like my backbone was his own*
*Darling, I know you can*
*Believe me when I tell you*
*you can love me like a man*
**– Bonnie Raitt**

Your wife's sexuality – *female* sexuality – is a harder thing to understand than your male sexuality, but here's one way to understand it: It's a lot like her body, with soft and lovely contours curling and curving all over the place.

This part of her body curves up into this part which slopes down to this other part which is now miraculously sweeping back up to this other part over here where it does a complete loop-de-loop and spirals down and swirls around to oh my god *this!*

She's all curves!

There's not a straight line on her!

She's got spheres and coils!

She's even got spirals!

And folds within folds!

Great God Almighty!

It's so multidimensional and curving and turning through so many planes at once, it's kind of dizzying, and you can spend a whole lifetime learning how to make love to it all.

And you do.

A good husband spends a lifetime learning all the planes and dimensions of his wife's sexual body, and also the planes and dimensions of her sexuality. She's a piece of work, this girl, and he *likes* the work, *loves* it, because the reward – a wife who feels completely sexually known by her husband and therefore completely sexually open to him – is heaven on earth for a man.

So you want to have sex with your wife? Great idea!

Now get to work.

The work is to know her.

For example, if you want to have sex with her, you might try asking yourself – or, better, her – does she want to have sex with you? How's she feeling physically? Is she tired? What kind of day has she had? When was the last time you fed and bathed the kids? What part of her menstrual cycle is she in? Which side of menopause is she on? How's she feeling emotionally? Is she in a good or bad mood? How's she feeling in the relationship with you? What's the latest nitwit thing you've done that you haven't apologized for yet? Is she stressed and busy? Is she feeling private and solitary today? Did you *already* have sex with her today, or yesterday, and maybe she's done with you, bozo? When was the last time you touched her *non*sexually, like just hugging, or a foot rub, or snuggling with her on the couch without heading for a breast? Have you *ever* touched her nonsexually? Are you keeping yourself healthy and fit and looking physically attractive to her these days? How's she feeling these days about her *own* body? Attractive? Sexy? Insecure? Shy?

In other words, is she up for it right now?

Go ahead. Figure it out. You can do it.

A word of caution: If the answers to the above questions add up to she doesn't want to have sex with you right now, don't even *think* about *blaming* her for that! And if she doesn't want to have sex with you right now and that archaic, sexist, misogynistic word "frigid" somehow makes it up into your mind and you actually *think* she's frigid, as opposed to the truth, which is that you're an insensitive *oaf,* I don't know if I can help you.

If the answers to the above questions add up to she *never* wants to have sex with you, if her sexual interest in you has just disappeared, here's what to do:

Find out why.

By asking her. By talking to her about it.

Don't get angry at her, don't turn away from her, don't reject her even though she's sexually rejecting you (that takes strength for a man!), but be her friend and stay her friend and keep gently inviting her to talk about herself. And don't always try to steer the conversation into sex; women hate that *("All he's interested in is sex! All he wants is sex!"),* and it'll get you nowhere. Let her take the conversation where she wants it to go. Remember that it's your interest in *her*, not just in sex, that feels intimate to a woman. So whatever you do, stay in relationship with her, and keep talking with her, and be her friend. Speaking as her friend, you could suggest that the two of you read some marital improvement books together, and talk; or go to a marriage seminar or workshop, and talk; or go to a marital counselor or sex therapist, and talk there. On the road to getting back to making love with her, there's going to be a lot of *talking* with her.

Remember that the sexuality of a woman is a high and holy temple that you may enter only through the labyrinth of her feelings about you, her feelings about men, her feelings about herself, her feelings about her body, her feelings about sex, the doctrines of her religion, the phases of her life, the phases of the moon, and her entire sexual trauma history with men, including you – all of it swimming around in a rather choppy sea of hormones that we men never even heard the names of.

You have to walk through the labyrinth with her. You really do. Don't worry about how long it may take. Just stay by her side and be on her side. There's no other way into the temple.

Female sexuality.

You have to learn it.

You have to earn it.

Whatever the state of your wife's libido, whatever her feelings, age, history, or mood, the best thing to do is to know that woman so well and respect her so deeply that your relationship with her is a work of genius, and then your wooing of her and your lovemaking to her, both in and out of the bedroom, will be a work of genius.

When you're making love to your wife in the bedroom, you pay attention to every curve and contour and dimension and plane of her beautiful female sexual body.

All you have to do now, in and out of the bedroom, is pay attention to every curve and contour and dimension and plane of what actually turns that beautiful female sexual body *on* – that's a lot of attention, but she's a *woman,* she's your *wife,* the girl is totally worth it.

A man's sexuality is a straightforward kind of thing, like a good hard fastball, but the great and amazing sexuality of a woman is all curves.

# Chapter 9

# TAMING THE WILD PHALLUS

*Hence it is that in men the privy member is disobedient and self-willed, like a creature that will not listen to reason, and because of frenzied appetite bent upon carrying all before it.*
**– Plato**

*This was the most unkindest cut of all.*
**– William Shakespeare**

On the night of June 23, 1993, in Manassas, Virginia, a woman named Lorena Bobbitt, wife of John Wayne Bobbitt, cut off her husband's penis as he lay sleeping after raping her when he came home drunk from a night of partying. She then took the severed penis for a drive around town and ended up throwing it into a field. It made all the news. She was excoriated by some, cheered by others, and a jury, after deliberating seven hours, found her innocent of any crime by reason of "temporary insanity and irresistible impulse."

I'll say.

I don't say I applaud or condone Lorena Bobbitt's action – just the thought of it gives me the complete willies, actually – but I understand where she was coming from. I'm sure many women in history have felt like cutting off a man's penis. Considering what men's penises have done to women over the course of history, how could they *not* feel that? In a moment of "temporary insanity and irresistible impulse" Lorena Bobbitt just took that feeling to the next step – to the cutlery drawer in the kitchen.

Here are two things everybody should know about the penis:

There's a very strong energy in it when it's erect. It's an enormously powerful and pleasurable energy that stirs and builds and grows and then just stands there, big and hard and urgent, and wants fiercely to be released. The energy itself doesn't much care *where* it gets released, it just wants release.

On a spiritual level, the energy in the penis has to be that strong because it is the energy of life itself, the energy of creation – genesis! – momentarily contained in the genital muscle of the male body and wanting to be released from that body into the genital space of the female body to generate more life. Life is enormously important to God, so He packed an enormously powerful and pleasurable energy into a rather – you should excuse the expression – *small* muscle of the human body called the penis which when put inside a vagina keeps creating more and more life.

Which is all well and good, but it leaves us men with half the creative energy of the universe parked in our poor little penises, and some of us are having a very hard time dealing with that.

The second thing everybody should know about the energy in the erect penis is that there's *so* much of it and it's *so* big and strong and urgent that unless it is tempered and tamed and held by something stronger than it – by *love* – it can go berserk. That's what rape and violence and killing and death and destruction and wars are: the energy in the penis – untempered, untamed, unheld by love – going berserk. When that energy is not a servant of love, it can become a servant of death, a weapon of death. That's why, aerodynamics aside, many of the weapons of death on the planet – knives, swords, spears, guns, bullets, bombs, torpedoes, planes, missiles, and rockets – look like big erect penises.

This is the paradox of the penis on this earth: When it's under control, it is beautiful, it is spiritual, it is divine. When it's out of control, it is terrible, it is demonic.

The task of every married man on the planet is to resolve the paradox of the penis by developing his capacity to love until the energy of his love is greater than and therefore in control of the energy in his penis. Not until he has accomplished this has he achieved true manhood. Once the energy of his love is stronger than the energy in his penis, the paradox of the penis is resolved, and the man is then free to use all the energy in his penis to serve love and life in the great and bounteous sex he's having with his wife.

It is very much in a man's self-interest to accomplish this. No man in his right mind wants his wife to cut off his penis at night while he's sleeping and take it for a drive around town. There are a lot better and more pleasurable things a wife can do with her husband's penis, and they *all* involve it remaining on his body.

# Chapter 10

## THE MARRIED PENIS:
## A FEW POINTS AND POINTERS

*A hard man is good to find.*
**– Mae West**

*You think it's easy having a penis?*
*You try having one. It's a lot of work*
*having a penis. A penis is a* problem!
**– A client to his wife in**
**a counseling session**

*See, the problem is that God has given men*
*a brain and a penis, and only enough blood*
*to run one at a time.*
**– Robin Williams**

So you have a penis. Which means you have a problem. And the problem is what are you going to do with it in your marriage? What part is your penis going to play in the sex with your wife?

What, for example, are you going to do with all the attention and focus you want on your penis during sex? What if your penis has a tendency to ejaculate too fast so the sex ends too fast and when you open your eyes your wife is scarfing down another Prozac and googling old boyfriends? What are you going to do about masturbation in your marriage? What are you going to do if your penis, because of some psychological or medical condition, or age, loses the erectile strength or reliability it used to have? If you have a penis, all these points arise.

So let me give you a few penis pointers.

## Penis Pointer #1

Don't sell it short. There are all kinds of articles and books and blogs out there telling us men that we should spread our sexuality around our bodies more; get more in touch with our non-genital, non-orgasmic, sensuous side; look for erogenous zones on our bodies other than our penises. Which is all well and good, but just in case you don't happen to find any, or the ones you do find are not in the same ballpark or even in the same solar system as the pleasures of your penis – if, frankly, you don't *care* about your other erogenous zones – don't forget to tell your wife that your penis is more than happy to stand in for all of them and basically you're good to go. Be honest with your wife about your sexuality, and be honest about your penis. I have often thought that an honest book written by an honest man about his sexuality and the role his penis plays in his sexuality would be a very easy book to write because not only would the *book* be titled ***Please Touch It***, all the chapters would be titled *Please Touch It*, and all the words in all the chapters would be "Please touch it." Rob Becker, in his one-man internationally acclaimed stage show *Defending the Caveman*, tells us about a guy who was getting a nice back massage from his wife one night in bed.

"How does this feel, honey?" she asked him.

He was silent for a moment. "About a foot and half away," he said.

There is so much sexual pleasure available to a man from his penis, so much sexual attention wanted by a man *toward* his penis, that a woman might not understand it – or maybe she understands it, she just might not believe it, because if you don't have a penis, the sexual attention it craves is – let's face it – pretty unbelievable. So get over whatever embarrassment you may feel and try to tell your wife about the immense amount of sexual pleasure you feel in your penis when she is touching it. It's hard to put into words, but try. On behalf of your penis, tell her the truth.

## Penis Pointer #2

If you ever have any problem with what they call premature ejaculation when you have sex with your wife, you can wait for my next book, *Up and Coming! A VERY Brief Look at Premature Ejaculation*, or, better yet, you can stop calling it "premature ejaculation" and realize that when it comes to the ejaculatory excitability of the penis, there's no such *thing* as "premature." Don't call it "premature ejaculation," call it intense sexual arousal that just suddenly blew its top. It's what penises do sometimes. The overwhelming, swift, uncontainable pleasure felt by your penis when it is near, next to, on, or – dear God! – *in* the body of your wife is totally natural, a testament to your love and lust for her, and a primal potency of your manhood.

It is estimated that what they call premature ejaculation happens to thirty to forty percent of adult males, though nobody knows for sure – for all we know, it could be a *hundred* percent – because no man in his right mind wants to talk about it.

There are books and articles and websites, techniques, therapies, and medications that can help a man who can't control his sexual arousal during sex with his wife, and you should avail yourself of any of them that you find helpful. Get whatever help you need – you'll be helping not only yourself but your wife whom you love and want to give great, strong, and long sex to. To the degree that your ejaculation problem limits your sexuality, it also limits her sexuality, and that's a problem for both of you, so the help you'll get will benefit both of you.

And while you're looking into all this, in some corner of your consciousness consider that your turbo-charged male sexual excitement problem may be yet another form – a subset, if you will – of your general male patriarchal self-centeredness problem in your marriage. We all have *that* one. Consciously or not, you may not be making *her* sexual desires, pleasures, and needs as important as your own. In essence, you may be *quitting* on her and abdicating your husbandly responsibility to sexually satisfy her.

If you're trying to be a good and generous lover to your wife and not leave her high and dry, disappointed, and deserted in the sudden cessation of sexual energy after one of your early orgasms *("I'm done, and so, therefore, are you"),* one very effective and very sexy and very loving way to control your sexual arousal during sex with your wife is to do things sexually to her and let her do things sexually to you that keep both of you in a state of pleasant and strong sexual arousal for a good long time – on a good night, it could be hours – until her state of sexual arousal, with you at the dials, grows and then erupts into her unbelievably powerful and beautiful orgasm, and then, after the roof settles back down on the house and you've gotten most of your hearing back, it's time for her to take your sexual arousal and grow it into your unbelievably powerful orgasm. Women have some *great* ways of doing that, you know.

And then you've *both* provided sexual satisfaction for each other and you're both done and very grateful, with rosy cheeks and very happy.

## Penis Pointer #3

To masturbate or not to masturbate as a married man. That is a question.

No right answer.

For some married men masturbation is a reliable and pleasurable release of the excess sexual tension that tends to build up in your mind and your penis – a kind of do-it-yourself hand-operated overflow valve – and by keeping your penis peaceful it can help keep your sexuality home, with your wife, where it belongs. For other men masturbation is a shameful secret compulsion, an addiction, something they want to stop but can't stop because it offers powerful, if momentary, relief from the boredom or anxiety or depression or self-hatred they go right back to feeling right after they're done. For some religious men it's "an intrinsically and gravely disordered action," a mortal sin, a form of adultery for a married man. Bible in hand, they recall what happened to poor

Onan after he masturbated – a cautionary tale if ever there was one. Then there are other men for whom masturbation is, "I've got a minute – and a hand – what the hell."

With such a wide variety of uses of and feelings about masturbation among men in this world, no one can prescribe to you what you should do about it in your marriage.

To masturbate or not to masturbate?

What *should* you do?

There's one thing you can do.

Ask your wife.

What does *she* feel about your masturbating? Does she care one way or another? Maybe she *likes* the thought of it; maybe she finds it erotic; maybe she wants you to tell her about it on the phone while *she* masturbates. Maybe not. Maybe she doesn't like it. Maybe she considers it a form of infidelity. Or maybe she's okay with it as long as she's your partner in the fantasy you're having during it. Then again, maybe she's okay with Marilyn Monroe. Or Lady Gaga. Or Myrna Loy. Maybe she thinks of your masturbation as a loss to her, a draining away of your sexual energy so less of it's available to her when she desires it; or maybe she thinks your autoeroticism leads to marital eroticism, that it's a firing-up of your sexual energy so *more* of it's available to her when she wants it. Maybe in her heart of hearts she doesn't want you feeling *any* sexual energy that isn't for her, because of her, toward her, and with her, but she's a compassionate woman, she understands the relief that masturbation provides you, so she's okay with it.

The point is that there is no way for a man to answer the masturbation question in his marriage without knowing his wife's feelings about it. So ask her. Have that conversation.

And ask yourself: How do *you* feel about masturbation as a married man? What *does* masturbation do to the sexual energy in your marriage? Does it subtract from it? Or does masturbation *add* sexuality to your marriage because it leaves you wanting a masturbatory fantasy of your wife to become your *real* wife – in the flesh – as soon as you can get to her flesh? Does your masturbation feel to you like fidelity – does it keep your mind on your wife and your sexuality toward her? Or does it feel like infidelity to you – does it take your mind off your wife and your sexuality away from her? Are you *addicted* to masturbation? Are you addicted to the pornography you use for masturbation? Does masturbation feel wrong or right to you? Or like no big deal one way or the other?

To masturbate or not to masturbate in your marriage? It's a question.

Ask it of your wife. Ask it of yourself.

From the authority of your heart, in the integrity of your manhood and the love of your wife, there will be an answer.

## Penis Pointer #4

What if you have erectile dysfunction? What if you're a younger man and for some known or unknown reason you're having problems getting or keeping an erection? What if you have some medical condition or take some medication that makes it difficult for you to get it up or keep it up? What if you're getting older and your penis is getting older and there's less and less energy stirring down there?

And then you're sitting there watching TV and you see the Viagra and Cialis and Levitra commercials, the ones where graying, handsome, virile looking guys are about to have sex with their pretty wives who are smiling sidelong at them as they walk up the stairs to the bedroom.

What should you do?

First, try not to feel ashamed, elderly, freaked-out, unmanned, or undone by it.

Good luck with that.

Second, get help.

The help you need might be psychological help from a therapist, or medical help from a doctor, or pharmacological help from a pill – or all of them – doesn't matter – just get the help you need – including the help you need from your wife in the form of her empathy, compassion, and uplifting sexual attentions. If you're 35 or 45 or 55 or 65, with firm resolve go to any lengths to preserve, prolong, and extend the erectile strength in your penis and the genital sexuality in your marriage. It is totally worth it.

There will come a time, however – like maybe you're in your seventies and it just isn't coming up anymore – when, with your arm around your wife whose own genital sexuality has probably waned as much as yours, you'll want to contemplate the great Zen *koan* that the great Willie Nelson announced on his 75th birthday – *"I have outlived my dick."*

# Chapter 11

# UNDERSTANDING MALE
# SEXUALITY:
# DESPERATELY SEEKING SOFTNESS

> *Then with a quiver of exquisite pleasure he*
> *touched the warm soft body. . . . And he*
> *had to come into her at once, to enter the*
> *peace on earth of her soft-quiescent body.*
> **– D.H. Lawrence**

> *I want to go back to bed and get inside her.*
> *That's the only time there's anything*
> *approaching peace.*
> **– Leonard Cohen**

You can't have the kind of great marital sex I'm talking about if you haven't gotten your sexuality under your control.

In order to get your sexuality under control so you can finally give it all to your wife so she can give all her sexuality back to you, you've got to try to *understand* your sexuality. When you understand something, you start to bring it under your control. Here's one thing I understand about male sexuality:

It is, primarily, a search for the quality of softness. It's a man looking for softness and peace and quiet on this earth and finding it in, with, or near the body of a woman.

Go ahead – think for a second about the physical attributes

of women that we men typically find sexual: skin, hair, lips, neck, breasts, arms, buttocks, thighs, vulva, vagina. Think about those for a second. . . . They're something to think about, aren't they? . . . What do they all have in common?

They're all *soft*. Her skin feels soft and smooth, her flesh is soft and yielding, and every part of her is curving along soft wavelike curves into every other part of her.

Behind all the sexual attraction, flirtation, manipulation, seduction, and intrigue, behind the immense amount of time, energy, thought, and money that goes into the whole *megillah* of male sexual pursuit and pleasure, we men are primarily looking for the soft parts of a woman's body. To a man's eye, a woman's body is an exquisite arrangement of soft, rounded, curving parts – the guy who carved the *Venus of Willendorf* knew *that* – and to immerse himself in all that softness, to lose himself in all that softness – to be *received* into all that softness – is at the heart of male sexuality.

We're probably talking about mommy here. The softness of a woman's sexuality is the softness that we knew, or should have known, first in our mother's soft womb and then next to her soft body at her soft breast. That's the archetype of softness we knew, or should have known, when we felt most welcomed and nurtured and loved by her, therefore most quiet and relaxed and secure inside ourselves. That's what the softness of a woman can give to a man. It's a lot. Even if you take all the sexism out of John Milton's explanation in ***Paradise Lost*** why God formed woman – *"For softness she and sweet attractive Grace"* – you've still got a sweet, attractive woman there whose softness is a divine gift of grace to a man.

I believe that the essence of male sexuality is a desire for inner peace, and a man's awed entry into the enfolding and nestlike softness deep in a woman's body leads to an inner peace deep in his own being.

This explains three things:

It explains a man's vexation and general desolation when his wife doesn't want to have sex with him, because when she doesn't offer him her sexual softness, he is cut off from his only known access to the peace inside himself. It is an achievement of mature manhood for a man not to get angry at his wife when she doesn't want to have sex with him, not even angry in the form of his silent and sullen withdrawal from her, but to stay open and present and loving and *nice*. A psychologically and spiritually mature man can do that because his journey through life has taught him that the peace and stillness he's looking for is not *really* in, with, or near the sexual body of a woman but in *himself,* and there are ways to find it that do not involve sex.

A male's search for softness and stillness also explains, in part, male sexual addiction. Actually, it *drives* male sexual addiction. The softness and quiescence of a woman's body that a man experiences during sex leads him to the softness and quiescence of his own being – *but only temporarily* – so to repeat that experience, the man repeats the sex, again and again, until he crosses a certain line and it becomes addiction, where the agains never end.

The search for softness at the heart of a man's sexuality also explains why marriage is the *best* place for a man's sexuality. If a big part of sex for a man is his total immersion in a woman's softness leading to an experience of inner peace and quiet and happiness, wouldn't it make sense for that man to have sex with a woman who knows everything about him, totally loves him, has committed her life to him, wants the best for him, and wants to give him everything she can to make his life wonderful, including all the sexual softness she has in all the breathtakingly beautiful places of her body where it is? That is sex at its best for a man, which is why sex is at its best in marriage.

If you get the marriage right, this is exactly what happens. If you give your wife the grace of your husbandly love, she will give you the grace of her wifely love, including the amazing grace of her sexual love. This is very good news about marriage and sex. It means you can have the best kind of sex within your marriage, sexually settled down into your marriage as you settle down into the sexual softness of your wife.

# Chapter 12

# MAKE YOURSELF SEXY
# FOR YOUR WIFE

*As a matter of opinion I think he's tops*
*My opinion is he's the cream of the crop*
*As a matter of taste to be exact*
*He's my ideal as a matter of fact*
**– Mary Wells**

*I put your leaves aside.*
*One by one: the stiff, broad outer leaves*
*The smaller ones,*
*Pleasant to touch, veined with purple;*
*The glazed inner leaves*
*One by one*
*Parted you from your leaves*
*Until you stood up like a white flower*
*Swaying slightly in the evening wind . . .*
*Where in all the garden is there such a*
*flower?*
*The stars crowd through the lilac leaves*
*To look at you.*
**– Amy Lowell**

It is fine for you to sometimes think of your wife as a sexual object and want her to be a sexy thing for you throughout your marriage, as long as you realize that *you're* a sexual object to her and are supposed to be a sexy thing too. That's one of the unspoken vows of marriage: *"Since I'm the only one you'll be having sex with for the rest of your life, I'm going to do everything I can to stay as sexy as I can for as long as I can."* Both husbands and wives silently take this vow. When it comes to sexiness in marriage, it's a total two-way street.

Some husbands understand that sexiness is a separate and equal responsibility in marriage, some don't. It's a foreign concept in patriarchy because it puts at least half the responsibility for marital sexuality on the male, and in patriarchy most of the responsibility for just about everything's that's actually or potentially wrong with the world, starting with original sin and including marital sexuality, falls on the female. In patriarchy, the girls are supposed to make themselves sexy – sexually attractive and sexually available – for us boys, thank you very much.

That, by the way, is Victoria's *real* secret.

But the times they are a'changin' and it's a new world, Victoria. In the new world, we married men are supposed to make and keep ourselves as sexually appealing to our wives as we want them to make and keep themselves sexually appealing to us. In the new world, it's no longer true that just because you're the man – the lord of the manor, the king of the castle, the entitled erection – you get to have sex with your wife when you want to. In the new world, you've got to be a certain *kind* of man – a sexually desirable man to your wife, one whose appearance *and* behavior are pleasure-giving and attractive to her, a sexy guy who gets her heart and all the rest of her throbbing. If you want to have good sex with your wife all your life, you've got to be that kind of man, and if you're not yet him, you've got to put in the effort and become him. It's like Shania Twain says,

*I need a man who knows how the story goes*
*He's gotta be a heartbeatin', finetreatin',*
*breathtakin', earthquakin' kind*
*Any man of mine . . .*

So if you look like a schlump or a schlepper, if you generally look like you just walked out of a laundromat, if you're lying on the couch flipping through so many channels on the TV that the only muscle in your body that can still get big and hard is the flexor pollicis longus in your thumb, forget it, man. You think that's sexy to her? You think she likes looking at *that?* You think that turns her on?

Rethink that.

And if you think you can behave like a jerk to her, that you can walk around the house all day in one of your world-class *moods,* irritable, unapproachable, completely unavailable, forget it, man. That's not sexy to her. It makes her afraid of you, which turns her off, and really mad at you, which turns her way off. When you behave like a jerk to her, when you're domineering and controlling, when you talk down to her, when you put her down and criticize or berate or belittle her, when you're dismissive of her and inattentive to her and you don't ever really talk to her, when you're completely unlikable, that doesn't make her want to take off all her clothes and lie down and have wonderful sex with you. A woman has to actually *like* you to want to have sex with you.

Go figure.

Just remember: If you act like a dick to her, your actual dick is the loser because it loses the privilege of her.

And another thing.

If you think that your giggling and sniggling about sex all the time like a twelve-year-old and your nimble-witted little gift for sexual puns and innuendoes are going to get her into bed with you, rethink that one too. Sexual silliness isn't particularly sexy to her. One day last winter I was stretched out on the bed reading while my wife was dressing to go out to dinner with some women friends, and she asked me if I would go start the car for her and turn on the heat and the seat-warmer.

I put my book down and looked at her looking at herself in the mirror. "You look *good*, honey," I said. "If you want to come over here for a second, I'm sure we could get the seat-warmer working."

"Har-dee-har," she said. "Not a chance. I'm in a hurry. And while I'm gone, see if you can make any progress on your lifelong journey out of junior high school."

My progress is slow, which is mostly okay because there *are* times when we both enjoy my pre-adolescent humor about sex — as long as I don't expect her to find it erotic, which works for me because she never does. Last week she told me that some friends of ours had just "signed the P&S" on a summer house down the Cape, so I, seizing the moment, said, "What?! They just signed a *penis?* They just signed a PENIS?!" and then took off on a three-minute completely extemporaneous and what I thought was totally hilarious flight of wit about signing penises: *"I wonder if they signed the penis in front of their lawyer."* . . . *"Did they notarize it?"* . . . *"Did they all sign the penis? Must have been one big penis!"* . . . *"How do you make a copy of a signed penis?"* . . . *"I'm glad I'm not a real estate agent signing penises all day." . . . "Did we sign a penis when we bought our house? Whose?" . . .*

And one more thing.

I hate to be the bearer of bad tidings, but pawing at your wife's breasts every time you see them under her blouse, pinching her bottom as the two of you are walking into a restaurant, or un-zipping your fly while she's sitting at the kitchen table trying to do soduko – those kinds of things aren't sexy to her.

Strange but true.

So what to do?

The thing to do is come to understand what *is* sexy to your wife, and then make yourself into a sexy thing for her.

Find a good time to talk with her and ask her, "What's sexy to you? How do you want me to look? What do you like me to wear? What kind of man do you want me to be that you'll be turned on to?"

And then listen to what she says. Ask more questions, and listen more. And then thank her and go off and think about it for a few days.

And then: *Do everything she told you to do.* Make every change she wants you to make. Become the kind of man she wants you to be.

She's shown you the way to her. So follow her way. It is literally the way *into* her.

Here's the way:

Look good to her. Look like you care about yourself. Look like you care about *her* and what her eyes have to see every day when she looks at you. Stay in shape. Go for a run, go to the gym, work out, take a walk, play your sports, get off your duff and *move*. Keep your muscles hard and strong. Get rid of that belly. Look healthy, energetic, and virile. You're a man. *Look* like a man.

Make yourself a handsome man. If you're not a natural-born Adonis, if the George in you is closer to Costanza than Clooney, still, do the best you can with what you've got. Wear clothes that make you look handsome to your wife. That sweatshirt you've been wearing since 1981, by the way, the one that made the Guinness Book of World Records for the "What Is He *Thinking?!*" category, is not going to get you into bed with her. What *does* she like you to wear? When it's time for sex with her, what does she like you to wear so she can have fun taking it off? Ask her about all that. Your two-day growth of beard? Ask her about that one too – in the meantime, shave. Your hair? Comb it.

And while you're combing, and shaving, and showering, and putting on that new polo shirt she bought for you and said you looked so good in, while you're making all this effort to look as good as you can for your wife, remember that with women, the sexiness of a man is about more than his looks. There's another side to it – it's the *kind* of man he is.

Try being this kind of man:

Be a nice man.

Be pleasant.

Be happy.

Be responsible.

Be respectful.

Be romantic.

Be truthful.

Be true.

Be her friend.

In a word, be a good husband to her. That's your best shot at having a great marriage, and having a great marriage is your best shot at having a lot of great sex in it.

A good husband. This is the kind of man a woman wants. If you're not yet him, become him. If you're already him, good for you. She'll like that.

You sexy thing.

# Chapter 13

# THE ONLY WOMAN FOR YOU

*Let thy fountain be blessed, and rejoice
with the wife of thy youth. Let her be as the
loving hind and pleasant roe.
Let her breasts satisfy thee at all times;
and be thou ravished always with her love.
And why wilt thou, my son, be ravished
with a strange woman, and embrace the
bosom of a stranger?*
**– Proverbs 5:18-20**

*When he is late for dinner and I know he
must be either having an affair or lying
dead on the street, I always hope he's dead.*
**– Judith Viorst**

A good husband is so completely sexually faithful to his wife that he doesn't think of it as sexually faithful. He doesn't think of faithful or unfaithful. He doesn't have those categories in his head. When he thinks of sex, he thinks of his wife, and that's the end of that.

Many men have to take a journey through various forms of unfaithful to get to faithful. *"Fidelity seems to come harder to us,"* says one writer.

Yup.

Actually, many men who are sexually unfaithful are sexual *addicts,* if you define addiction as an energy inside you that operates outside your control, and if you define *sexual* addiction as the uncontrolled directing of sexual energy – *in any form and to any degree* – to any other woman than your wife.

In our culture this directing of sexual energy to women other than our wives hides under quasi-benign euphemisms like "dalliance," "harmless flirtation," "fooling around," "playing around," "messing around," "making a mistake," "cheating," and "straying;" and the man who strays is called quasi-benign names like "ladies man," "libertine," "philanderer," "womanizer," "woman chaser," "skirt chaser," "rake," "wolf," and "playboy" – but it's anything but benign.

It's infidelity.

The sending of sexual energy to women other than your wife could be anything from having sexual intercourse with another woman, to sexual touching, to flirting, to catching the eye of the pretty woman on the train, and all the other times you can't keep your eyes off women, including all the pornography you look at in all the places it is, which is pretty much everywhere.

All of it's infidelity.

All the little seduction games you play with other women? All your sexual shenanigans?

Infidelity.

Anything you might say in defense of these behaviors is, at best, delusion, and, at worst, dishonesty – in either case, bullshit – so save your breath.

Just listen:

Be completely sexually faithful to your wife, which means that every aspect, element, feature, form, part, and degree of your sexual energy gets directed *exclusively* to her.

There is no exception to this.

To whatever degree and in whatever form your sexual energy is directed to another woman than your wife – whether it's your neighbor, or your secretary, or colleague, or your friend's wife, or that waitress leaning over the table with the cleavage, or the half-naked actress on the movie screen, or the bar girl on the beer ad, or just a cute little thing that you spot on the street – *that's* it, right *there, that's* infidelity, and hurts your wife deeply (believe me, she sees it *all)* and pisses her off royally, so cut it out.

Lose the concept of "another woman." In any form she appears. There is no other woman. For all your sexuality, the only woman is your wife.

It's really important that you understand this. Once and for all, *get* this fidelity thing.

Recently I heard a story about a woman in New Hampshire. She was forty-seven, married for twenty-five years to the same man, with three college-age, well-adjusted children, a good wife and mother and neighbor and citizen, a good woman living a comfortable and happy life.

Then she found out her husband had been having an affair for the past three years with the town librarian.

She hung herself in the garage.

This is not a story about a woman's problem with codependence or depression. And it's not a story about a weak woman. It's a story about the enormous effect that a husband's infidelity has on a wife, the rotten betrayal it is, and the devastation it causes.

She hung herself.

Get it now? Get what marital infidelity does to women inside?

Fidelity!

Leave all women, except your wife, alone!

So here's what to do:

Being really honest with yourself, identify all the behaviors you're involved in where your sexual energy – *in any form and to any degree* – is directed toward a woman other than your wife. This other woman might be an actual person in your life or she might be an electronic image on your computer screen or a photograph on a billboard you see every day on your way to work.

What women and what parts of women are your eyes looking at? What women are you talking to, or e-mailing or texting, and what's going on in all those words? What other women besides your wife are you touching, and why are you touching other women besides your wife?

What do you do, by the way, when the *Victoria's Secret* commercial comes on the TV? How long do you stand in the drugstore leafing through the swimsuit issue? Where are your eyes as you sit sipping coffee in the café?

Being really honest with yourself, check it all out.

And then cut it all out.

Right now.

Here's how:

Right now remember a time recently when your eyes strayed to a woman other than your wife. In your mind's eye look at her. Look at all the parts of her that you like looking at. Go ahead, look at her . . .

Feel the urge to *keep* looking at her. That's a strong urge, isn't it?

*But hold it right there* – at the level of urge. Don't let it get to the level of behavior. *Don't* keep looking at her. Look away. Look down.

I *said,* look down!

Good going.

Now go back to what you were doing.

This is strength. This is manhood. This is a man's love for his wife.

*"True love,"* says a sage, *"focuses one's heart completely on the beloved. Then, one does not want to look at another; in fact, one does not look at another. If he does, he has not found love, he is only kidding."*

Stop kidding. Focus your heart completely on your wife and become a faithful husband and a true lover of her.

It's a magnificent energy, your sexuality – the crest jewel of your manhood – but only when it's with your wife.

Fidelity!

# Chapter 14

# THE MYTH OF THE YOUNGER WOMAN

*I need to be bold, need to jump in the cold water*
*Need to grow older with a girl like you . . .*
**– Joshua Radin**

*There is no old age. There is, as there always was, just you.*
**– Carol Matthau**

Two more points about fidelity, especially for you older guys whose wives are aging.

Point 1: Schmuck, you're aging too.

Point 2: The fact that your wife is aging (or, for you younger guys, that she is someday *going* to age) does not constitute a loophole in your promise to be faithful to her. Just because you live in a culture that seriously devalues women as they age, belies their beauty and sexual vitality, and keeps showing us movies where the aging male star is having romantic love and/or sexual adventures with an actress half his age – you don't get to be in that movie! The fact of your wife's aging is not your license to leave her, cheat on her, or otherwise betray her for some pretty young thing. So stop all that stuff.

One time a client of mine named Eliot, a fifty-five-year-old attorney in a Boston law firm, came in for his morning session looking troubled.

"I'm a mess," he said. "Angie and I are doing a lot better these days, and she's still the finest woman on the face of the earth, but you know what, Robert? She's getting *old*. She's got a couple of those age spots on her face now, and she's letting her hair go all gray, and when I look at her hands, they look *old* – lined and wrinkled like an old lady's. Meanwhile there's this paralegal on the fourteenth floor who's incredible – beautiful! – she actually looks a little like Angie at that age. Anyway, we were alone in the elevator together the other day, and I swear – "

"Don't do what you're thinking of doing, Eliot," I said.

"What am I thinking of doing?" he said.

"Something so incredibly dumb and morally wrong," I said, "that I'm going to fight you every step of your stupid way to it."

Your wife may be a youthful 21, or 31, 41, or 51, and physically she may be cute as a button, pretty as a picture, drop-dead gorgeous, or beautiful beyond compare.

Whatever.

It's not gonna last.

This woman is going to *age*. That's the reality. Everything physical about her will change. Her skin, hair, hands, breasts, her face and figure – it's all going to age right before your very eyes.

It's like the great stripper Gypsy Rose Lee once said, *"I've got everything I've always had. Only it's all six inches lower."*

It's going to happen. You ready, Freddie?

No? Well, *get* ready.

Because if you use the fact of your wife's aging to leave her for a younger woman – or to let your sexual energy, in any form and to any degree, be directed to a younger woman – you're a jerk.

No offense.

But if you did take offense, let me try to say it another way:

If you use the fact of your wife's aging to leave her for a younger woman – or to let your sexual energy, in any form and to any degree, be directed to a younger woman – *you're a total asshole.*

Grow up. In this world there are certain things you do and certain things you don't do, and one of the things you don't do is discard the woman who has given you *everything* – her hand in marriage, her trust, her body, her youth, babies – her *life,* man – and you don't dump her, you don't just discard her, you don't throw her away because she's getting older and some nubile young thing happens to be jogging down your street with her breasts jiggling.

That's called *abandonment,* pal – betrayal, a double-cross! – and you just don't do it.

Don't you get it? There's *always* going to be a younger woman than your wife jiggling her way down your street. Plenty of 'em. A whole new crop of pretty young things jiggles up every year. Whatcha gonna do? Go jogging with them *all?* Don't be an idiot. Forget about it. Stay home with your wife.

Love that wife of yours so deeply, madly, truly that when you look at her and see the aging in her, the gray in her hair and the lines in her skin, when you see that older face and that older body, you change the prescription of your glasses and see all that as beautiful. It's not that you won't see that stuff – you will – but you'll see it as beautiful. And it *is* beautiful, if you're seeing it right. It's the beauty of an older woman. It's the beauty of the younger woman you wed, now grown older, still her, still in love with you, still woman, still *your* woman, still beautiful.

*There is no old age. There is, as there always was, just her.*

That's what I'm talking about.

It's called marriage. It's called love.

And it goes both ways.

Marion Woodman, the great Jungian psychoanalyst from Toronto, remembers this moment in her marriage:

*"We had been married twenty-five years. It was early morning. I had awakened cranky and discontent. I was sitting in the living room drinking my coffee, thankful for silence. Then he decided to get up and make his own breakfast. I saw him in the kitchen trying to break an egg into a single little egg poacher. He was in his old Black Watch housecoat, his two spindly legs sticking out the bottom. 'I deserved better than this,' I thought. But as I watched him patiently cutting his bread, there was something about the concentration of his hand on the loaf that caught a lifetime in a moment. 'He's still here,' I thought. 'I'm still here. We're in this little box on the seventeenth floor in a place called Toronto with a crazy world out there. Whatever life is, we've walked our parallel paths together. God knows, I've made him suffer, and he's made me suffer. But we're here. Neither of us has given up the search.' I respected him. Whatever the mystery is that holds two people together exploded through my heart. Aware of my old housecoat and not so thin legs, I knew that human love and divine love are of*

*the same essence."*

Love like that.

They say beauty is only skin deep. I say that for a good husband – a true lover – there's a beauty that's deeper than skin deep, and that's the beauty you see when you look at your wife. It's the beauty of the woman you married, your wife whom you love, the life that you've shared, the heart she entrusted to you forever. It's the fact that she knows you better than anyone on this earth will ever know you, and cares for you and loves you to a depth that no pretty young thing could even conceive of, jogging, jiggling, or not.

When you look at your wife, your heart overflows with such love of her that there *are* no younger women because there are no *other* women, there is only *one* woman, there, standing by the bed, with gray in her hair now, eyes tired perhaps but bright and filled with love of you, smiling at you, light all around her, the most beautiful woman you have ever seen or *will* ever see.

*"Do not admire the beauty of other women,"* says Leo Tolstoy, *"but live with the one to whom you have become united, and do not leave her."*

Got it?

Just in case you don't, if you're having any last thoughts of being with a younger woman, if you're so freaked-out by your own age that you're trying to hide from it in the arms of a woman who's a younger age, if you think you want to go in the direction of that stupidity and that perfidy, then right now go to a full-length mirror, take off all your clothes, and stand there and look at yourself.

Go ahead, take a good look . . . head to toe . . . take a good

look at yourself . . .
    Hello?
    Are you kidding?
    Are you *crazy?*

# Chapter 15

# THE SEVEN CIRCLES OF SEX: ATTRACTION, ADDICTION, AND BEYOND

> *Okay,*
> *dear ones, are you ready?*
> *Are you braced?*
> *Well then:*
> *Who can hear God sing*
> *if that dog between your legs is barking?*
> *Who can hear God sing*
> *if that canine between your*
> *thighs*
> *still*
> *wants to do circus*
> *tricks?*
> **— Hafiz (*trans. Ladinsky*)**

To some men, women are like a kind of drug – alluring, exciting, intoxicating, and irresistible. The woman might be one of those "Dear-god-give-me-a-break" women walking by on a beach in a bikini, or any woman anywhere. When these men see a woman, they become a little crazed inside and can't keep themselves from sexually looking at her and/or sexually pursuing her in the hope of sexually enjoying her. Many men are addicted to women in this way, and many married men are addicted to women in this way. Even when these men want to stop these behaviors, even when their behaviors are completely destroying their careers, their marriages, their families, and their lives, these men can't stop. This is sexual addiction, even though in our culture we don't call it that, we call it boys-will-be-boys-ha-ha-ha.

Underneath the adrenaline gush, the ego rush, the phallic flush, and the thrills and chills of a married man's sexual addiction to women, including his addiction to pornography, there sits inside the man some kind of emotional pain. It may be the pain of loneliness, or sadness, or anxiety, or disappointment with life or himself, or it may be the pain of growing older – but there's always emotional pain underneath sexual addiction. Any man who wants to once and for all *break* his sexual addiction has to look at his inner pain and work it down small enough so that he's not being driven to stupid, dysfunctional, dishonorable, and immoral sexual acts by it anymore.

Becoming completely conscious of one's emotional pain so that it's not driving our sexuality anymore – to pull those wires – is doable – actually, not *that* difficult – but how many men are going to do it?

Right.

So there's got to be another way.

There is. There's a way through male sexual addiction. It's easier than looking at one's inside stuff because it involves looking only outside at one's *behavior,* and changing that. To find the way out of male sexual addiction, a man needs to take a journey in through the seven concentric circles of sexual behavior. We can *behave* our way out of sexual addiction.

Each circle, starting with the farthest one out and moving toward the center, represents a less and less engaged form of sex with a woman other than your wife, a weaker and weaker form of the addiction; and by the time you get to the center circle, you are free of sexual addiction to women, and all forms of your sexual interest, engagement, and behavior are now with only your wife.

Let's take a trip in through the seven circles.

In the seventh circle, the farthest one out, there are no controls at all on your sexual addiction to women. You see a woman, she's attractive to you so you're attracted to her – attracted so strong it's like a *tractor* pulling you to her! – and so you approach her, and then if you have to, you follow and pursue her, you do your little mating dance around her, play all your games and make all your moves on her, until you get her, she's yours, whereupon you touch her, you have sex with her, and then you pull up your pants and close the door on your way out. At this level of sexual addiction, there are no restraints, no rules, no boundaries, no marriage vows, no morals. When you are acting out in this circle, there are hardly any *thoughts*. If you have a career, there is no career. If you have a high and responsible position, there is no position and no responsibility. If you have children, there are no children. There is certainly no wife. There is no consideration of consequences at all. For married men who are acting out in the seventh circle, there is only the addiction.

So you pull yourself together a bit and move in to the sixth circle. In the sixth circle, you see a woman, you're attracted to her, you want her, you approach her, you follow and pursue her, you get her, and you touch her, but you now have one rule: No intercourse. You won't put your penis into her vagina. You're Mr. Clean now, and you restrain your touching to hugging, kissing, holding, patting, petting, stroking, and the ten thousand other forms of sexual touching that stop short of intercourse and sometimes pretend *not* to be sexual touching, as in, "I did *not* have sex with that woman!" or, "Would you like a back massage?" In the sixth circle, you'll still sexually touch her, but you've gotten a little control over yourself now, and you've drawn a line or two.

Now you move in to the fifth circle. In the fifth circle, you see her, you're attracted to her, you want her, you approach her, you follow and pursue her, and you still get her, but when you get her, you won't touch her – you're done with that – but you'll *talk* to her. Oh boy, will you talk to her! There she is, across the room at a party, a bar, a hotel lobby, a faculty tea. You go over and start talking to her. You charm her. She talks to you. You get to know her, draw her out, gaze deeply into her eyes, turn up the charm, say all the right words. Using only words, the two of you engage the gears of your two sexualities, and, turning on talk, you begin the beguine. The fifth circle is the flirtation circle. It's *very* crowded. All emotional affairs – extramarital affairs that do not involve sexually touching another woman but through the intimacy generated by words always involve inappropriate emotional connection, subtle sexuality, and your growing dependence on another woman for needs that only your wife should be meeting – all emotional affairs, whether they are conducted in person, on the phone, in e-mails or texts, or on Facebook are in this circle. If, like most men, you're good at deluding yourself, you can feel relatively innocent in this circle, but there is sexual attraction and sexual intrigue and sexual energy every step of the way. Many married men have a hard time knowing or admitting that they're flirting with a woman – they call it "just being friendly." If you're a married man and you want to know when you're flirting with a woman, ask your wife, who usually has to stand there silently witnessing the whole sorry scene, feeling like screaming and/or killing you.

So you better hurry up and move in one more circle, to the fourth circle. In the fourth circle, you see a woman, you're attracted to her, you want her, but you won't approach, pursue, or talk to her. The only thing you'll let yourself do now is look at her. And boy, do you look at her! In this circle, the whole addiction is crammed into your eyes. You'll look at her, stare at her, eye her, ogle her, furtively glance at her, and get a big libidinal thrill every time you catch her glancing back at you over the cheese dip. Sexuality is played out between the two of you with your eyes. The fourth circle is a relatively benign one, the engagement with the other woman is milder than in the other circles, but like all the other circles, it's still seduction and it's still addiction and it still makes your wife, who is again silently witnessing the whole show, feel like screaming and/or killing you.

So you move in to the third circle. In the third circle, you spot a woman, you look at her, you're attracted to her, you feel the familiar wanting of her . . . so you don't look at her again! That's right, you heard me – *you don't look at her again.* You couldn't help the first look – that's usually involuntary, an accident, a twist of fate, a social call from karma – but you don't allow yourself a second look. You look away. You look down. You leave the room. If necessary, you leave the conference, or the country. Your eyes are under your control now. You've got the addiction contained inside your own being now, so it no longer shows up outside your being in your behavior. In this third circle, you might still think about the woman or fantasize about her – both of which are forms of looking at her in your *mind's* eye – but you can't look at her with your physical eyes anymore because you know that's not right and you don't need that anymore. Then you'll be like the great 13th-century Sufi poet-saint, Jalaluddin Rumi, who said in one of his poems, *"For years I gave away sexual love with my eyes. Now I don't."*

When you're strong enough and disciplined enough and wise enough and in love with your wife enough and *married* enough to not need to look at another woman a second time, you're almost there. Now you move in to the second circle. Here's what happens in the second circle: When you see a woman, you still notice her physical appearance as an interesting phenomenological event in your sensory field – *here she comes . . . she's pretty; she's plain . . . she's 28; she's 98 . . . and there she goes* – and that's the end of that. She was just a figure on the far horizon of your conscious-ness, a momentary flashing forth of a familiar cognition of no great importance to you anymore. You witness the brief flashing forth of the phenomenon inside and then you witness its cessation and then you witness the next phenomenon flashing forth inside you, and so on. Life goes on. Oobladi, ooblada.

And now you're ready to step into the first circle, the

innermost circle, which is the complete cessation of sexual addiction. In the innermost circle, you look at a woman and you see her as a human being among seven billion other human beings on the planet. You see human beings as human beings now. Their size, shape, age, color, and gender have ceased to matter to you. Whoever happens to make their momentary cameo appearance in front of your eyes, your response is the same: In your heart you are friendly, in your words and actions and looks you are courteous and respectful, and in your mind you are quiet. You have been on a long and winding road through the seven circles of your sexuality, and you are finally bringing it all back home to the one who has been waiting all this time for you in the center – your lovely wife.

# Chapter 16

# RECOVERING FROM INFIDELITY:
# THE FOUR PILLARS

*Woman, please let me explain*
*I never meant to cause you sorrow or pain*
*And let me tell you again and again and*
*again – I love you*
**– John Lennon**

*Because you're mine*
*I walk the line*
**– Johnny Cash**

If you've already transgressed and been unfaithful to your wife, in the recent or distant past, consider the rest of your marriage and the rest of your life to be a time of redemption for you. With some wives there can be no redemption – the transgression was too much, too often, or too sordid, the betrayal too deep – but with some wives redemption is possible. Your best shot at total redemption is based on four things, the four pillars on which you are trying to rebuild the temple of your marriage. The four pillars are:

## I

Never ever do it or anything remotely like it again. Be a completely faithful husband to the end of your days, and let all your actions, behaviors, and words be continuous and irrefragable evidence of your fidelity to your wife for the rest of your life.

## II

Understand that your infidelity was and will always be a major emotional trauma to your wife that she carries very deeply in her being, and it will occasionally surface in her being as sadness, hurt, distrust, and anger – at you – possibly for the rest of your life, and you have to be a man and get okay with that, understand that you caused that, you earned it, you sowed the wind and you reap the whirlwind. There will be many whirlwinds over the years, emotional storms that arise out of your wife, triggered by a memory, by a name, by a song on the radio or a smell in the weather, by nothing at all. Sometimes she'll cry and want you to hold her, sometimes she'll want to yell at you, interrogate you, punch you, sometimes she'll want to have nothing to do with you. Most of it will feel unfair to you, but it's not. It's the pain you put into the marriage with your infidelity coming back at you, and it's completely fair, and you have to love her through it all.

## III

When you feel remorse, apologize. And when the feeling of remorse strikes again and the moment feels right, apologize again. Remorse is what a good man feels when he has done something wrong to somebody, and an apology that has true remorse in it is emotionally and spiritually healing for both the wrongdoer and the wronged. An apology is an act of honesty, generosity, humility, and courage. It is a form of love. It balances the account. Apologies with sincere remorse in them can, with time, win a wife's forgiveness, and, I hear, God's.

# IV

Think of the rest of your marriage and the rest of your life as redemption, and think of that not as a burden or emasculation or a mark of shame but as a great opportunity, a way to remember that you want to be and are now spending your life trying to be the best husband you can possibly be to your wife. From now on you're trying to square it with her, make it right with her, so from now on you're on your best behavior to her – always being kind and nice and helpful and faithful to her – and one day, with you redeemed and your marriage restored, your wife is back to where she once belonged, where she's always belonged, sitting alone on the throne of your heart.

If you've already been unfaithful, rebuild the temple of your marriage. It is the most sacred temple on earth – your marriage and your family. Rebuild it on the four pillars.

# Chapter 17

# THE SEXUAL DISCIPLINE
# OF THE MARRIED MAN

*Give me a man who is man enough to give himself just to the woman who has wed him.*
**– Sienna Miller, playing Francesca Bruni in the movie *Casanova***

*The sun became full of light when it got hold of itself*
*Angels only began shining when they achieved discipline*
**– Jalaluddin Rumi**

I'm not saying that marital fidelity or the journey through the seven circles is easy. It's not. It requires discipline. Discipline isn't that easy. That's the bad news.

The good news is that discipline is one of the strengths – the virtues – of adult manhood, so those of us who have achieved adult manhood or who want to achieve adult manhood have already embraced discipline as part of the deal. All our male heroes – soldiers, the policemen and firemen of September 11th, great athletes, successful businessmen, or common men who get up every morning and go to their jobs to provide for their families – all our male heroes and exemplars do it through discipline. A man doesn't achieve manhood until he achieves discipline.

Discipline is power – over yourself. Discipline is when you don't do everything you feel like doing, and you sometimes do things you *don't* feel like doing, because you finally figured out what you *really* want to be doing in your life, which is to live your life as a mature, disciplined, virtuous and virile man.

Sexual discipline is the power to say no to any of your sexual impulses, urges, desires, attractions, or arousals that happen inside you before they travel outside you – outside your jurisdiction – as sexual behaviors and actions that are going to badly hurt all the ones you love and possibly ruin your life.

Sexual discipline for a married man is the power to hold *all* his sexuality inside himself and inside his marriage, where it belongs, and not let it go outside his marriage, where it never belongs. You have to stop all that. Listen to Rumi writing a letter to his son who is having an extramarital affair:

> *"Many have made the same mistake. When they get where they think they want to be, they find nothing. They're just far from their wives and children, and dying of thirst, these riders and their horses. Realize this and stop. Even fools learn how to stop. Don't do it! Don't! Don't! That's all."*

This takes strength. All forms of discipline take strength. Married sexual discipline – the complete and absolute containment of a man's sexuality within his marriage – takes a lot of strength.

It takes a lot of strength because you're a man, and being a man, many sexual impulses, urges, desires, attractions, and arousals toward women other than your wife will come up inside you. There's one of those women over there right now, at the gym, on the street, by the check-out, in the office every day in the cubicle behind you. She's attractive. She's pretty. She's got nice legs. You want to look at her, talk to her, be alone with her, be entranced by her. You want to touch her. You *want* her. What can you do?

There are a few things to do. The first thing to do is don't worry about any of that stuff coming up inside you. It happens. It goes with the territory of being a man. Charges of that energy will come up. Sometimes they're little charges, sometimes they're big charges, sometimes they're bolts from the blue. Until you've gone through the seven circles, it's part of the deal of being a man. It's called wanting. Don't worry about the wanting.

The second thing to do is get ready for a struggle – a real tussle – because when the sexual impulses, urges, desires, attractions, and arousals toward women other than your wife arise in you, when the wanting comes, it's going to slam into the solemn promise you made years ago to your wife – and to your family and your friends and your community and your God – to always be a true and faithful husband to your wife, forsaking all others and being sexual only with her until death. It may be a small and easy struggle for you, or it may be a great and arduous struggle. It's different for different men. Don't worry if it's an arduous struggle for you.

Just make sure you win the struggle.

Here's why it's completely in your self-interest to win the struggle of sexual discipline in your marriage:

If you spill ten gallons of gasoline on the ground and ignite it, all you'll get is a single big violent meaningless explosion; but if you take the same ten gallons of gasoline and run it through the fuel injectors and cylinders of an automobile engine, you'll get a very long series of controlled – that is, disciplined – explosions that will take you all the way to where you want to go. By containing and harnessing and focusing the energy, you strengthen its purpose and increase its power. Sexual discipline for a married man is the containing and harnessing and focusing of your sexual energy completely within your marriage, so that instead of dissipating your sexuality with women other than your wife, you give it all to her, so she gives you all of her sexuality, and that's a lot of sexuality being exchanged in a very sexual marriage.

Explaining why there is discipline in the religious life, the French saint Thérèse of Lisieux, who was a cloistered nun from age fifteen to her death at twenty-four, said:

*"Consider the oaks of the countryside, how crooked they are; they thrust their branches to right and left, nothing checks them, so they never reach a great height. On the other hand, consider the oaks of the forest, which are hemmed in on all sides; they see light only up above, so their trunk is free of all those shapeless branches which rob it of the sap needed to lift it aloft. It sees only heaven, so all its strength is turned in that direction and soon it attains a prodigious height."*

I am one hundred percent certain that St. Thérèse did not mean this as a phallic image, but I'm sure she wouldn't mind if I run with it a little to make my point: If you discipline your sexuality, if you hem it in on all sides by your marriage, if you turn all its strength in the direction of your wife, it's going to grow big and tall and straight and lift aloft to a proud and prodigious height. It won't be like a shapeless oak of the countryside; it'll be a towering oak of the forest. Really good wood.

There's another reason why it's completely in your self-interest to maintain sexual discipline in your marriage:

Because you're trying to achieve manhood. Manhood is when you know what's the right thing to do in life, and you do it. Being completely sexually faithful to your wife is the right thing to do in your life, and you know it – so you do it.

And here's a third reason why it's in your self-interest to win the struggle for sexual discipline in your marriage:

There is an immutable law on this earth: Actions have consequences. It's the law of karma, God's law, and you can find it written in all the world's spiritual literature: *"And I will recompense them according to their deeds, and according to the works of their own hands."* (Jeremiah 25:14) . . . *"Be not deceived; God is not mocked: for whatsoever a man soweth, that shall he also reap."* (Galatians 6:7) . . . *"Each man shall reap the fruit of his own deeds."* (Koran 6:165) . . . *"There is no place in the universe, no mountain, no sky, no ocean, no heaven, where one does not undergo the consequences of actions performed by oneself."* (Yoga Vasishtha, II:29:7)

Actions have consequences. Here are some of the possible consequences of your having sex with a woman other than your wife:

Destroying your reputation. Losing your job. Losing

everyone's respect. Breaking your wife's heart. Losing your marriage. Losing your children. Losing everything you hold dear in your life. Lifelong regret and guilt and shame and self-condemnation. Loneliness. Emptiness. Universal disorder.

You want any of that? Actions have consequences on this earth, and extramarital sexual actions have grave consequences.

When the extramarital temptations come – and they will come; the culture we live in is one big long extramarital temptation – also remember this: Your children are watching everything that you do. You are the model on which they model themselves for their whole lives. Model manhood for them. Model your virility. Model your great achievement for them.

Sexual discipline in marriage. It's an achievement of manhood.

# Chapter 18

# EIGHT DAYS A WEEK:
# THE DIMENSIONS OF MARITAL SEX

*He has sprouted; he has burgeoned;*
*He is lettuce planted by the water;*
*He is the one my womb loves best. . . .*
*My eager impetuous caresser of the navel,*
*My caresser of the soft thighs,*
*He is the one my womb loves best.*
**– Inanna**

*Pillowed on your thighs in a dream garden,*
*little flower with its perfumed stamen,*
*singing, sipping from the stream of you –*
*sunset, moonlight – our song continues.*
**– Ikkyu Sojun**

So you've done some good work on your sexuality and your marriage. You've healed some of your sexual wounds and corrected many of your misconceptions about sex. You're coming to understand both male and female sexuality on their physical, emotional, and spiritual levels. You're finally thinking straight about sex. And you've got your sexuality under your control now, so that you're giving all of it to your wife, and she, bless her heart, now wants to give all of hers to you too.

So now you're ready for great sex in your marriage.

Good man. Good going.

So what is great sex in marriage?

Great sex in marriage is whatever you and your wife want it to be now that you're both connected to each other in love. The particular forms of sex that you and your wife create together – the sexual practices you engage in, the things you like to do with each other and to each other and for each other – will be unique to you and are for the privacy of your own bedroom (or living room, or laundry room) and for the privacy of your own hearts. Remember that the trust and love and goodwill and intimacy you need to generate between you for great sex in your marriage can be generated *only* in private, between only the two of you, alone, in the *sanctum sanctorum* of your marriage. Nobody else is allowed into that. Don't even talk about it with anybody.

While you're at it, send the dog downstairs too.

So it's evening and you're finally alone with each other and tonight's the night and you're all showered and shaved and looking handsome and sexy for her and she's wearing that blue or pink or red or black lingerie you love and looking gorgeous and sexy for you, and her scent is sweet and redolent, and the lights are low, and the stereo's on with the birds chirping away in the Brazilian rainforest, and you close the bedroom door and for the next few hours the two of you have marital sex.

Here's what can happen in the sex between you and your wife during that time. Here are the eight dimensions – the *energies* – of great sex in marriage. In a good marriage on a good night, marital sex can be: *Procreation* (optional) . . . *Play* . . . *Gift* . . . *Sanctuary* . . . *Connection* . . . *Desire* . . . *Worship* . . . *Love.*

\*\*\*\*\*\*\*

## Sex as Procreation

*Every living thing has this procreative, or*
*sexual, energy in its make-up, for it is*
*the Creative Energy of God manifesting*
*on the physical plane of creation.*
**– Bhai Sahib**

*And God blessed them, and God said*
*unto them, Be fruitful, and multiply.*
**– Genesis 1:28**

God seems to be a great lover of life. He created life and wants the luxuriant earthly garden that He created teeming with life, including human life. So God gave everybody, including humans, sex, and the exquisite ecstatic pleasures of sex, to get us all into bed to have sex and produce more and more life. If procreation is your purpose, God has made it your pleasure, so go, be fruitful, and multiply – knock yourselves out.

\*\*\*\*\*\*\*

## Sex as Play

*We are seas mingling, we are two of those*
*cheerful waves rolling over each other . . .*
**– Walt Whitman**

*License my roving hands, and let them go*
*Before, behind, between, above, below . . .*
**– John Donne**

Let's face it, marital sex is *fun*. Two people who like each other a lot close their bedroom door and start talking and joking and dancing and touching and hugging and kissing and one thing leads to another and they spend the next couple of hours having the time of their lives with each other. They have fun together. They fool around. They play. They take off all their clothes and disport around the room doing spontaneous, impulsive, frolicsome, and frisky things with each other. They're like children playing, making a world together. It feels good. It feels great. Great marital sex is when two people – two kids who *really* like each other – go to one of their favorite playgrounds – their bedroom – and play with each other for hours.

*******

## Sex as Gift

*When I get that feeling I want sexual healing.*
*Oh, baby makes me feel so fine . . .*
**– Marvin Gaye**

When you love somebody, you want to give them things. When you love somebody in marriage, you want to give them sex. Sex makes a great gift in marriage, and you can give it for lots of reasons. You can give your partner sex because he's feeling kind of down today and could use a little pick-me-up. She's not feeling well physically and you know a way to make her feel a little better for a while. She's not liking herself today and you want to show her how much *you* like her – *love* her – by *making* love to her. He's feeling bad today – *really* bad – about himself, his work, his life – about any of the things life is so good at making us feel bad about – and you know a surefire way of making him feel *really* good. He's given you a wonderful gift recently, or a whole lifetime of wonderful gifts, and you want to give him sex as your way of saying, "Thanks, honey." She's had a success in life, or an achievement, or a stroke of good fortune, or been given some kind of recognition from the world, and you want to give her a little something yourself to celebrate the occasion. It's his birthday, or anniversary, or Valentine's Day, or Father's Day, or Bastille Day, or Groundhog Day, or Labour Day in New Zealand (October 26, ladies), or International Migratory Bird Day (May 9), and you want to give him sex as a present. Or you want to give him sex for no reason, just because you love him and you have a few moments, just because you looked across the room and saw her standing there and your heart filled up with wanting to do something nice for her. The marital gift of sex can be long or short, his or hers or both of yours, depending on the need, the time, and the kids. Also, since marital sex doesn't cost any money, it's a very good gift for couples on a budget.

*******

## Sex as Sanctuary

*But one unto him*
*Will softly move*
*And softly woo him*
*In ways of love.*
*His hand is under*
*Her smooth round breast;*
*So he who has sorrow*
*Shall have rest.*
**– James Joyce**

*"Come in," she said, "I'll give you*
*shelter from the storm."*
– **Bob Dylan**

Great marital sex is a kind of sanctuary we can go to when we have need of sanctuary.

We all have need of sanctuary. It's a pretty crazy world out there, and we all go out into it every day and come back home from it carrying with us, inside us, all the world's craziness and intensity and tension and sorrow, and we periodically need refuge from that, we need sanctuary, a shelter from the storm, somewhere to lay our head, feel soothed and comforted, and rest. Great marital sex is a place of great rest.

*The room is dark and warm. Your bodies are dark and warm. You turn your body to her body. Her flesh smells sweet, like musk, and faintly burning. You flow out toward her body until your body finds her body and you settle deeply in, folding fierce and fetal into the flesh of her body, your body getting smaller, your mind quieter and quieter. You have found the soft and fragrant female body you've been searching for, a sanctuary of pleasure and peace, and so you breathe in deeply, make a small sound in your throat, and you stay there where it's dark and it's warm and it's quiet and you're soothed and you're safe and you let out a long breath and you rest.*

\*\*\*\*\*\*\*

## Sex as Connection

*And the closer I'm bound in love to you*
*the closer I am to free.*
**– Indigo Girls**

*Oh, what a night! hypnotizing, mesmerizing me!*
*She was everything I dreamed she'd be!*
*Sweet surrender, what a night!*
**– Frankie Valli**

In a good marriage where there is a strong connection between the husband and wife, the sexual relationship is connected to all the other parts of the relationship. A man's doing his share of housework and childcare, meeting his wife for lunch at the mall, their phone calls or voicemails or e-mails or texts to each other, their conversation at dinner, their walk around the block in the evening – the warm smiles, looks, words, touches, and kindnesses – the warm hearts that radiate between them during the day ignite the sex that burns in their bedroom at night. In a close marriage, the whole relationship is a long rolling wave of human connection that frequently rises into spectacular erotic connection. In such a marriage, everything you do with each other, everything you say to each other is a form of your sexual love. And the sex – truly connected sex between a husband and wife whose marital connection is the center of their lives – is amazing sex. It's an incredible interaction, a mutual exchange of giving and receiving pleasure of such immense power over the two of you that there's nothing for the two of you to do but surrender your sexual bodies to each other. And when it's over and you're all dressed and feeling warm and cozy and going back into your own lives, though you're disconnecting physically, you're more connected than ever.

*******

## Sex as Desire

*He loves your sexy body*
*He loves your dirty mind*
*He loves when you hold him*
*Grab him from behind . . .*
*Every time he touches you*
*His hair stands up on end*
*His legs begin to quiver*
*And his mind begins to bend*
**– The Traveling Wilburys**

*I'm so excited!*
*And I just can't hide it!*
*I'm about to lose control*
*and I think I like it!*
**– The Pointer Sisters**

There's a raw and primitive energy in us that is of the body and drives us to have sex with another body. There's a carnal appetite in us, a dark, focused, fixed hunger, ancient and animal, crouched, still. You can see it in the set face and the narrow purpose in the eyes staring at you from the marriage bed. Being engulfed in that energy can be a little frightening. All your controls come off and out pour looks and words and doings and imaginings and a swirling Möbius strip of two bodies gliding and sliding over each other that is a wonder to behold. The sheer power of it makes it a little embarrassing to speak of afterwards as you're eating cookies in the kitchen, thinking, "What the hell was *THAT?!*" It was desire, a kind of confession married people make to each other in the dark cave of their hunger for each other. It was sexual desire, a wild, exuberant form of their love for each other.

*******

## Sex as Worship

*I always feel the need for a feeling of worship in lovemaking.*
– **Alice Walker**

*With this Ring I thee wed,*
*With my body I thee worship . . .*
– **Book of Common Prayer**

Great sex in (heterosexual) marriage is Woman worshiping Man, and Man worshiping Woman. It is the mutual celebration and adoration and interpenetration of the two primal energies in the universe. When a married man and woman enter their bedroom for sex, they are entering a sacred place, and what happens there is a ceremony of worship. The man worships the Woman of circles and spheres and curves and coils, and the woman worships the Man of hard muscle and pulse and sinuous and strong lines. There is gesture and movement – a slow choreography – and absolute stillness at the heart of it. It is worship, and adoration, and awe, one energy in the universe genuflecting in a kind of stunned ecstatic silence at the revealed vision of the other energy in the universe. On this level, great sex in marriage is mutual and simultaneous rapture.

*******

## Sex as Love

And if you want love, we'll make it
Swimming in a sea of blankets,
Take all your big plans and break 'em
This is bound to be a while . . .
— **John Mayer**

Making love with you
left me peaceful, warm, and tired.
What more could I ask?
There's nothing to be desired.
— **k.d. lang**

"*The true spiritual nature of love cannot be defined or described,*" says the ancient sage Narada. Love is too out there, too mystical and mysterious to be put into words. But, says a modern sage, there are ways to give earthly form to this love. The forms of love on this earth are: courtesy; kindness; friendliness; gentleness; tenderness; generosity; altruism; goodwill; benevolence; compassion; empathy; respect. To exhibit these virtues toward another person is love. Love is all about another person – in everything you do, in everything you say, in everything you think and feel, you do it for the benefit of the other person. You want to make life easier for them, you want to please them, you want to help them, you want to help them feel good about themselves, you want to give them everything you've got to make them feel good. In marital sex, you want to make your partner feel good all over. When two married people are having sex and each is completely devoted to making the other feel good – because they're in love and because their sex is an expression of their love – that is loving marital sex, that is lovely sex.

*******

In a good marriage on a good night you get to all these energies of sex (and more – you and your wife can add your own), and the two of you move from one dimension to the other and back again – again and again – circling and circling with each other on currents of sexual love that only the married can ride.

# Chapter 19

# PLAN B:
# WHAT TO DO IF YOUR
# MARRIAGE ISN'T SEXY

*Is sex necessary?*
**– James Thurber**

*There are two birds of golden plumage,
two inseparable friends who dwell on the
selfsame tree. The one eats the sweet and
bitter fruits thereof, and the other looks on
calmly, in silence.*
**– Mundaka Upanishad**

Does the frequency and the quality of the sexual relationship between a husband and wife matter in a marriage? Does *sex* matter?

There are two answers to that question – yes, and no.

Here's the yes:

Yes, sex matters in a marriage! Are you kidding? This whole book is about the yes! Marriage is both a private and public avowal of the deep and passionate love that two people feel for each other, and marital sex is a private transaction – a corporealization – of that love between them, a reciprocal exchange of love between betrothed lovers that not only celebrates the love they feel for each other, but creates more of it – they are, literally, *making* love. The physical intimacies of marital sex combine with the intellectual, moral, emotional, and spiritual intimacies of marriage to form the deepest, nearest and dearest intimacy there is on this earth between two people, which is perfect marriage. Loving marital sex is also one of the all-time best stress-reducers known to humankind, free, portable, legal, respectable, repeatable, with no known side-effects except, afterwards, a little rubescent glow about the face and neck and an irresistible urge to eat Oreos.

So does sex matter? Is it important in a marriage? Of course. Marital sex is the *nectar* of marriage. It is the ecstatic energy that explodes from the fusion of two souls in marital union. The sweetness of their sex is a major part of *la douceur de vivre*, the sweetness of their life.

So go for it. Do everything you can think to do – including everything I've told you to do in this book – to have good sex in your marriage. Marital sex is a very high proceeding, so proceed.

That's the yes. That's Plan A.

And here's the no. Since the no directly contradicts the yes, you'd better get your mind ready for paradox.

*"The test of a first-rate intelligence," says F. Scott Fitzgerald, "is the ability to hold two opposed ideas in mind at the same time, and still retain the ability to function."*

Now you're ready for paradox.

Here's the no. Here's Plan B.

Sex really doesn't matter all that much – in marriage or anywhere else. It's a nice thing, and it's certainly necessary for the propagation of the species, and if you had your druthers you'd probably want to have it in your marriage as opposed to not having it; but it's really not *that* big a deal and it's not *really* necessary, which is actually good news if you're in a marriage where you don't have your druthers about sex.

What if you're in a marriage where the sexual connection isn't very strong, or frequent, or good, and often leaves one or both of you feeling frustrated, hurt, resentful, sad, and alone? Or what if one (or both) of you is carrying around sexual abuse from your past – any form or degree of sexual inappropriateness and boundary violation that has been perpetrated on you – which has left you with an aversion to sex, a repulsion for it, or a fear of it so strong that you're basically done with it in this life and your spouse has been forced to be done with it in the marriage? What if sex – libido – just isn't a strong energy you feel within yourselves or toward each other? What if it never was, or once was but isn't anymore? What if it's just not part of the deal in your marriage now?

(If you're getting on in years, be careful here. Just because your libidos are not what they used to be, just because they're quieter in there, that doesn't mean that sex has quit in there and it's over in your marriage. It probably means that, given your age, and hers, spontaneous sexual energy – sexual arousal that arises readily, heatedly within you at a look, a touch, a kiss, a thought – is not anywhere near what it used to be (and may not be anywhere near *anything* anymore); but the capacity to enjoy both the giving and receiving of sensual and sexual pleasure *is* still in there, in both of you, so the two of you just have to get creative and figure out how to call it up from each other, how to summon it forth, how to *induce* it in each other now. When you're getting up there in years, that fire may not be flaming anymore inside either of you, it's probably *banked* now, not a bright burning flame but a glowing ember – not quite as hot maybe, but hot enough and smoldering with all the years of your love for each other – and that sexual ember needs some special attentions to fire it up into actual sexual behavior between the two of you. Now your sexualities are jewels more deeply set in your bodies, but they're still beautiful, and fun to play with, and worth the finding. So try to find them. Set aside an evening a week for the two of you to sit down or lie down together and talk. Wear something with sexual possibility. Talk intimately – about yourselves, or your marriage, or the current events of your lives, about anything under the sun, including how you're feeling about lying there next to each other with sexual possibility. Be okay with whatever she or you are feeling about that. If you're feeling amorous and aroused and sexual, great. If you're not aroused, tell each other the kinds of special attentions you think might help to induce that energy in you, to *get* you aroused. Is there something you want to see? Say? Touch? Ask for? Is there music you want to hear? A dance you want to have? What might relax you? What might help you move from the intimacy of talk into the intimacy of touch? Whatever works for you, whatever works for her, do that. Sometimes nothing really works right away; sometimes – because in a few minutes it's going to be worth it – you just force yourself. Whatever you do, whatever you need done to you, is fine. The point is to *try.* When the years are building up and the sexual fires are burning down, until they burn *out* don't give up on sex – though it won't be the same exact sex you had with each other in earlier years, it's the same sweet making love with each other, and if now you have to make an effort to get there, you make the effort.)

But what if you don't get there? What if you've tried *everything* to get sex going in your marriage, but the only place it's gone is further south? What if you and your wife have read every marital self-help book and sex manual on the shelves; googled all 296,415,128 sex advice references on the worldwide web; talked to every therapist, cleric, clairvoyant, and tantric crackpot in town; gone to seminars, workshops, weekend encounters, Caribbean retreats, and high-priced hotel suites with gilded mirrors on the ceiling and a Jacuzzi burbling merrily in the bathroom – and still no sex? What if you've tried teddies, dildoes, vibrators, handcuffs, inflatables, and every sexual massage oil on the market, including the Amorous Avocado Passion Potion from the Balinese rainforest – and still no sex? What if both of you are popping Cialis, ExtenZe, Provestra, and Spanish fly gelcaps like crazy; and you've tried every sexual position the two of you could get into without major ligament damage; and you've both read every article on sex that has ever been published in all the women's and men's magazines in the world, including, in <u>Cosmo</u>, *"Bring-It Breasts: How to Use Yours to Drive Him Crazy!"* – what if you've read all this and done all that and still the sex between you is nonexistent, infrequent, or I-hope-this'll-be-over-before-CSI-at-10?

And what if, though there's little or no sex in your marriage, the two of you still love each other and want to stay in the marriage?

What to do?

Plan B.

Make sex of no great importance in your marriage. The way to do that is to make sex of no great importance in your mind.

This can be done by any person of any age for any reason at any time, you included. And it can be done on two levels – the relational level and the spiritual level. It works best if you do it on both levels at once.

On the relational level, if you've tried everything and sex still isn't one of the forms of connection in your marriage, if it just doesn't seem to work in the relationship, do everything in your power to make every other form of connection in the relationship *really* work. Companionship. Caretaking. Friendship. Conversation. Compassion. Loving service. Support of each other. Enjoyment of each other and the life you're sharing. Don't think of the sex that's not there in your marriage, think of all the nice, intimate connections that are there, and keep making those connections, and know that by making them the two of you are being intimate and are making love. And remember: Though there may be no great ardor between you, there can still be lots of affection – you can touch, and hug, and hold, and caress, and comfort each other, and give each other foot massages and head and neck and shoulder and back massages, and you can talk with each other and laugh and cry with each other about everything, and then you can fall asleep next to each other holding hands. When you have all these forms of connection in your marriage, even if there's not a strong sexual connection, you have a strong marital connection and a good marriage that feels good, like sex, but with less hassle, and fewer Oreos.

On the spiritual level, if sex is not one of the pleasures of your marriage, if it's less than sensational or less frequent than you'd ever thought possible and still have the will to live, try this: If the desire for or the idea of sex happens to come up inside you but the time or place or your or her mood or your or her anatomy or any condition of body or mind or circumstance of life is saying no – no sex for you right now – don't get mad at anyone, don't flip out, and don't get so bummed out that you ruin the whole day or wreck the week for everybody in the family. Don't do that. There's a different choice you can make. You *have* a choice. It just takes a second to make it, and you make it.

If the desire for or the idea of sex with your wife comes up, you don't try to suppress it – it's a fact: the thought of sex *did* come up, you *do* have that desire for her – so you let it come up, and if you know or you're told that you can't act on that desire this time – that your *idea* of sex is not going to become the *act* of sex this time – and you're left with some bad feelings inside about that, you let those feelings come up too – the rejection, the anger, the hurt, the loneliness; they're facts too – you let it *all* come up, you *watch* it all come up, you go to the place inside you from which you can watch all your feelings and desires coming up inside you without having to act on any of them.

It's a choice you make. It's a stepping back in to a different place inside you. It's a kind of discipline. It's the same discipline athletes practice when they play through pain, or soldiers when they fight through fear, or any strong person when their desires and feelings are telling them to do one thing but they know they have to do a harder thing. It's a form of manhood. Spiritually it's the power to remember that while desires, feelings, fantasies, thoughts, and all the other matters of the mind are rising and falling within you, you're the one who stays still, watching them all.

*"The one you are looking for is the One who is looking,"* says St. Francis.

That one – that One – is you. *You're* the one who's looking – from inside. You're the watcher, the witness of it all, the spectator. When you remember that, you can watch everything that comes up inside you, including sexual desire, without having to do anything about it. In that place the quietness is so quiet and the peace passeth understanding, so nothing, including sex – or no sex – is that big a deal.

Sometimes in marriage we see each other in the kitchen and we like what we see so we hug and kiss and get turned on and run into the bedroom and throw off all our clothes and jump into bed and have great sex. Sometimes we don't. Sometimes it's not like that between us. Sometimes we're the bird in the tree tasting the sweet fruit all around him – a busy little pecker – Plan A – sometimes we're the bird in the tree sitting still, calmly watching – bird of paradise – Plan B. The two birds are inseparable friends sitting close together on the selfsame tree, and they're both of golden plumage and having a good time.

# Chapter 20

## LET'S GET IT ON

*You're the cutest thing I ever did see*
*I really love your peaches*
*want to shake your tree . . .*
**– Steve Miller Band**

*Tonight's the night!*
*It's gonna be alright!*
*'Cause I love you, girl,*
*Ain't nobody gonna stop us now . . .*
**– Rod Stewart**

A good husband feels sexual desire for his wife. Lots of it. And *only* for her, exclusively, for all your years together.

Till the two of you are too old for desire.

But until then . . . sexual desire.

The kind of desire that when you see her – her face, her lips, her hair, her curves – you want to move to her and touch her, to kiss her, to move forward to her and reach for her, everything in you rising to her, rising up to her.

And when you do reach her and touch her and rise up to her, when she rises up to you, somewhere inside you you're still sixteen and going, *"Oh, thank you! Oh, thank you! Thank you! Thank you!"*

That kind of desire.

So you go to her and tell her she's the cutest thing you ever did see, and the prettiest, and the sexiest, and the most gorgeous and the most delicious, and the most scrumptious and sumptuous and voluptuous, and you can't wait to get into bed with her and . . .

You feel all that for your wife, and you tell her.

And she feels it for you.

And then you're dancing in the darkened living room to Marvin Gaye's *"Let's Get It On"* . . .

> *If you feel like I feel, baby*
> *then come on . . .*
> *oh, come on . . .*
> *Let's get it on . . .*

All evening long . . . gettin' it on . . .

Lucky man!

Married man.

# AFTERWORD:

# AN EARNEST APPEAL TO WIVES

*When you say a back rub means only a*
*back rub,*
*then you swat my hand when I try,*
*well, now, what can I say*
*at the end of the day –*
*"Honey, I'm still a guy."*
**– Brad Paisley**

*Stay, lady, stay*
*stay with your man awhile*
*until the break of day*
*let me see you make him smile . . .*
**– Bob Dylan**

I hope you're having great sex in your marriage. I hope it's fun for you, and frequent, and fulfilling, and I hope your youthful interest in sex has stayed with you (with adjustments for age) throughout your marriage. And I hope your husband likes sex as much as you do and you're having all the good sex you want in your marriage.

If that is not the case, if you're not getting good sex in your marriage, if sex with your husband has not been good for you and so your interest in sex is going, going, or has gone, or if your sexuality or his is drifting outside the marriage, do not attribute that to the inevitable attrition of sexual intimacy alleged to be inherent in marriage, attribute it to the unresolved personal sexual issues you and your husband brought into the marriage, attribute it to the emotional disconnection that exists between you and your husband in the marriage, and attribute it to a general incomprehension of and invalidation of female sexuality in the world, including in your marriage. Since all of that gets addressed in this book, and since your husband has read it or is reading it or is going to read it after you give it to him to read, there is hope for the sexual future of your marriage. And if, after your husband reads this book he reads my other book on husbanding, *Good Husband, Great Marriage*, and learns how to achieve truly intimate relationship with you – learns how to create the great marriage I'm talking about in that book – I think the two of you have a very good shot at achieving intimacy, excitement, and fun in the sexual part of your marriage.

While he's doing everything he can do to improve the marriage (mainly by improving himself), if you've already lost a lot of your interest in sex (or sex with *him*), do everything you can to revive it. Even if you think you don't want to. I'm asking him to do things in this marriage for the sake of the marriage that he doesn't think he wants to do, and I'm asking you to do the same, and for the same reason – for the sake of the marriage.

You're in a *marriage.* Sex is important in a marriage. Marital sex is a beautiful expression of your appreciation and admiration and affection and adoration of each other. It's a generous gift of great pleasure and deep relaxation to a person you love. The consummate closeness of marital sex makes it easier for the two of you to be close in other parts of your marriage. Sex is very important in a marriage because the sexual union is the furnace in which the marital union keeps getting forged.

Not only are you in a marriage, you're in a marriage to a *man.* Sex is very important to a man. It's an acceptably manly way of feeling open and vulnerable and strong and proud and playful and passionate and connected with a woman; it's a sanctuary from the rough and tumble workaday world a man has to go out into every day; it's a fitting reward for all that he does for you and the family, for the good man that he is; it's your loving welcome of him into your life, your heart, your very body; and it feels better to a man than anything you can possibly imagine.

So don't give up on sex. It's important to him, so make every effort to make it important to you again. Start to talk to him about your sexuality more honestly than you ever have. *Teach* him your sexuality, how it *really* works. Teach him that your sexuality spans the whole erotic spectrum of sensitivity and sensuousness and sensuality and lust – from talking to each other in gentle tones, to taking walks together holding hands, to snuggling on the couch watching reruns of *Love Boat,* to hugging and kissing in the hallway for a moment, to foot massages, back massages, all over your body massages, all the way up to the two of you making wet, wild love to each other half the night. If you think it's needed, get him to go to marital therapy with you, or sex therapy, or get yourself into individual or women's group therapy, and talk about your sexuality there. When the time feels right, bring your husband into the bedroom with you and get the lights and the music and the clothes just right, just the way *you* want them, and then, by prior agreement, teach him what feels good to you by telling him when it does feel good and by stopping him when it's not feeling good and trying to get the poor guy back on track.

Don't give up on sex. In the past, sex with your husband may have been anything from disappointing to boring to irritating to infuriating, and once it goes dormant in a marriage it can be a difficult thing to get going again – and it may take a while – but do your best. Marital sex is worth it. It's a good thing. At its best it's a great thing. Sex is a great gift given to all of us by God, who gives us marriage as the best place on earth to enjoy it.

A word to you wives:

Sex.

Good sex in a good marriage.

Great sex in a great marriage. Your sexuality and his sexuality in the private garden of your marriage.

Sex with a married woman.

He's going for it.

You're the married woman.

You go for it with him.

# ACKNOWLEDGMENTS

My mother Sylvia gave me a love of words and an appreciation for great writing. My father Jack is my model of manhood. Both my parents taught me precision. My mother-in-law Yvette teaches me courage and a completely unsinkable enthusiasm for life. My friends give me their affection, their great company, their guidance and wisdom, and laughter. My daughter and her husband and our three granddaughters are the precious jewels and the joys of my life. My wife is the amazing grace of my life, my touchstone of truth, editor in chief, and the most beautiful woman I have ever seen. Whenever I am writing about marriage, or love, or the beauties or virtues of woman, I am writing about her.

Rob McQuilkin and Ed Walters (for your perfect representation and hard work on behalf of the book); Morris Rosenthal and Kirby Hamilton (for the generous gift of your time and advice); Meghan Tillett (for the release); Fred Courtright (for the permissions); Donny Kaplan (for taking the handoff and running with it into the world); Zick Rubin (for your wise counsel and your belief and encouragement); and Jane Alter (for your great, incisive, persevering editing until the writing was right) – thank you all for everything you did to get this book to publication. You have all been kind.

A special thanks to our cousin Odessa Sawyer, an extremely talented artist and wonderful young woman, for the cover design and illustration.

A wonderful thing that happened to this book on its way to publication was Jenny Chava Hudson, the owner and publisher of Merrimack Media, and artist – she transfigured the manuscript into the book, designed and produced the book jacket, created the beautiful website (www.sexwithamarriedwoman.com), and totally respected the collaboration with us, so it came out right.

Gurumayi, Baba, and Bade Baba – thank you for your grace, your protection, and your love.

# NOTES

## DEDICATION

King Solomon, The Apocrypha

Sting, "Fields of Barley"

## INTRODUCTION

p. i: Salt 'n Pepa, "Let's Talk About Sex"

p. i: Ralph Waldo Emerson, The Heart of Emerson's Journals, January,1850, p. 247

p. i: Zsa Zsa Gabor, Take My Wife, ed. Hugh Payne, Black Dog and Leventhal Publishers, New York, 2008, p. 141

p. ii: Good Husband, Great Marriage: Finding the Good Husband . . . in the Man You Married: A Relationship Revolution, Grand Central Publishing, NY, 2007

## CHAPTER 1 – MARRIAGE: THE BEST SEXUAL POSITION

This chapter and chapters 5, 7, 8, 13, 14, 20 and the Afterword were originally published under different titles in my book Good Husband, Great Marriage by Robert Mark Alter, with a foreword by Jane Alter. Copyright © 2006 by Robert Mark Alter. By permission of Grand Central Publishing. I have revised them all for this volume.

p. 1: Marvin Gaye and Tammie Terrell, "If I Could Build My Whole World Around You"

p. 1: Jo Stafford, "Make Love to Me"

## CHAPTER 2 – THE VARIETIES OF MARITAL SEX: THE BAD, THE GOOD, AND THE SNUGGLY

p. 5: Billy Joel, in The Book of Italian Wisdom, ed. Antonio Santi, Citadel Press, 2003, p. 62

p. 6: Pointer Sisters, "Slow Hand"

p. 8: *"Gonna find my baby, gonna hold her tight, gonna grab some afternoon delight,"* Starland Vocal Band

## CHAPTER 3 – THE GROUND RULES FOR A TRULY SEXUAL MARRIAGE

p. 9: Bob Dylan, "Precious Angel"

p. 9: I have borrowed the image of a woman's body being a wonderland from John Mayer's great song, "Your Body Is a Wonderland."

p. 13: This description of the chivalrous knight is borrowed from Maurice Keen, Chivalry, Yale University Press, New Haven and London, 1984, p. 30 and *passim.*

pp. 13-14: Elizabeth Gilbert, Eat, Pray, Love: One Woman's Search for Everything Across Italy, India, and Indonesia, Penguin, NY, 2006, pp. 309-313

p. 16: *"Let my beloved come into his garden, and eat his pleasant fruits."* Song of Songs, 4:16

p. 18: *"Not tonight, dear, I have a concussion."* I borrowed this line from a caption on a cartoon by Michael Crawford, in The Complete Cartoons of The New Yorker, ed. Robert Mankoff, Black Dog and Leventhal Publishers, NY, 2004, p. 637.

p. 20: *"God has a very big heart . . . and he will not go,"* from the film *Zorba the Greek*

## CHAPTER 4 – THE HEALING POWER OF MARITAL SEX

This chapter was originally published in my book How Long Till My Soul Gets It Right? (HarperCollins, 2001) under the title "Sexual Wreckage." I have revised it for this volume.

p. 21: Rainer Marie Rilke, Letters to a Young Poet, transl. M.D. Herter Norton, W.W. Norton & Co., NY, 1934

p. 24: *"Remember that one of God's intentions for marriage is for repair of all forms of human wreckage, and that includes
sexual wreckage."* The concept that God, or Nature,
intended marriage to be a place where the childhood
emotional wounds of both partners get healed came
to me from the writings of Harville Hendrix. See especially his Getting the Love You Want: A Guide for
Couples, HarperPerennial, NY, 1988. I have not been
able to find the source of Dr. Hendrix's quote that I use
as an epigram to this chapter; I think it's something he
said in a taped lecture.

## CHAPTER 5 – THE GAUNTLET: YOUR WIFE'S SEXUAL HISTORY

p. 27: Jean Baker Miller, "Connections, Disconnections, and Violations,"
Stone Center Working Paper #33, Wellesley Centers for
Women, Wellesley College, Wellesley, Massachusetts

p. 27: Bob Dylan, "Love Minus Zero/No Limit"

## CHAPTER 6 – BECOMING A BETTER LOVER

p. 31: Big Bill Broonzy, "How Do You Want It Done?"

## CHAPTER 7 – UNDERSTANDING FEMALE SEXUALITY: EVERYTHING IS FOREPLAY

p. 35: Bonnie Raitt, "Meet Me Half Way"

p. 37: Sappho, in The Quotable Woman, Running Press, Philadelphia, 1971

## CHAPTER 8 – CONNECTING WITH YOUR WIFE'S SEXUALITY: FOLLOWING HER CURVES

p. 39: William Blake, "The Marriage of Heaven and Hell," in The Po-
etry and Prose of William Blake, ed. David Erdman,
Doubleday and Co., Garden City, NY, 1970

p. 39: Bonnie Raitt, "Love Me Like a Man." Words and Music by Chris Smither. © 1970 (Renewed) EMI U Catalog, Inc. All rights controlled by EMI U Catalog, Inc. (Publishing) and Alfred Publishing Co., Inc. (Print). All Rights Reserved. Used by Permission of Alfred Music Publishing Co., Inc.

## CHAPTER 9 – TAMING THE WILD PHALLUS

p. 45: Plato, The Timaeus, transl. Francis MacDonald Cornford, Bobbs-Merrill Company, Inc., New York, 1937, p. 357

p. 45: William Shakespeare, Julius Caesar, III, 2, 183

p. 47: *"When that energy is not a servant of love, it can become a servant of death, a weapon of death."* In Hebrew, the word for "penis" and the word for "weapon" (zayin) are the same. See Sam Keen, Fire in the Belly: On Being a Man, Bantam, New York, 1991, p. 95. In the military, soldiers distinguish their weapon from their penis by chanting, *"This is my rifle, this is my gun, one is for killing, the other's for fun."*

## CHAPTER 10 – THE MARRIED PENIS: A FEW POINTS AND POINTERS

p. 49: Robin Williams. I found this quote on the web.

p. 53: *"For some religious men it's an intrinsically and gravely disordered action."* Cathechism of the Catholic Church, #2352

pp. 53-54: *"Bible in hand, they recall what happened to poor Onan after he masturbated – a cautionary tale if ever there was one."* Genesis 38:8-10.

p. 56: *"I have outlived my dick."* I found this quote by Willie Nelson on the web; don't know if it's apocryphal.

## CHAPTER 11 – UNDERSTANDING MALE SEXUALITY: DESPERATELY SEEKING SOFTNESS

This chapter was originally published under the title "The Essence of Male Sexuality" in my book How Long Till My Soul Gets It Right? (HarperCollins, 2001). I have revised it for this volume.

p. 57: D.H. Lawrence, Lady Chatterly's Lover, Wilder Publications, New York, 2009, p. 73

p. 57: Leonard Cohen, "The End of My Life in Art"

p. 58: *"For softness She and sweet attractive grace."* John Milton, Paradise Lost, Book IV, line 298

p. 59: *". . . and there are ways to find it that do not involve sex."* For some of those ways, see my book How Long Till My Soul Gets It Right? (HarperCollins, 2001), especially the sections "The Mind," "Meditation," and "The Inner Place."

## CHAPTER 12 – MAKE YOURSELF SEXY FOR YOUR WIFE

p. 61: Mary Wells, *My Guy*

p. 61: Amy Lowell, "The Weather-Cock Points South," in Caroline Kennedy, She Walks in Beauty, Hyperion, NY, 2011, p. 32

p. 62: *"If you want to have sex with your wife all your life, you've got to be that kind of man, and if you're not yet him, you've got to put in the effort and become him."* I have tried to describe this kind of man at length in Good Husband, Great Marriage.

p. 63: Shania Twain, *Any Man of Mine*

## CHAPTER 13 – THE ONLY WOMAN FOR YOU

p. 69: Judith Viorst, "True Love," in It's Hard to Be Hip Over Thirty, and Other Tragedies of Married Life, World Publishing Co., NY, 1968

p. 69: *"Fidelity seems to come harder to us."* Sam Keen, Fire in the Belly: On Being a Man, Bantam, NY, 1991, p. 222

p. 73: *"True love focuses one's heart . . . he is only kidding."* Swami Muktananda, Satsang 4, SYDA Foundation, South Fallsburg, NY, p. 101

## CHAPTER 14 – THE MYTH OF THE YOUNGER WOMAN

p. 75: Joshua Radin, "I'd Rather Be With You"

p. 75: Carol Matthau, Among the Porcupines: A Memoir, Turtle Bay Books, NY, 1992

p. 76: Gypsy Rose Lee: *"I've got everything I've always had. Only it's all six inches lower,"* in Barbara McDowell and Hana Umlouf, Woman's Almanac, 1977

pp. 78-79: Marion Woodman, *"We had been married twenty-five years. . . . I knew that human love and divine love are of the same essence."* The Ravaged Bridegroom, Inner City Books, Toronto, 1990, p. 211

p. 79: Leo Tolstoy, *"Do not admire the beauty of other women, but live with the one to whom you have become united, and do not leave her."* The Gospel in Brief, transl. Isabel Hapgood, Dover Publications, Mineola, NY, 2008 (1893), p. 41

## CHAPTER 15 – THE SEVEN CIRCLES OF SEX: ATTRACTION, ADDICTION, AND BEYOND

This chapter was originally published in my book How Long Till My Soul Gets It Right? (HarperCollins, 2001) under the title "The Seven Circles of Sexual Addiction." I have revised it for this volume.

p. 81: Hafiz, "Who Can Hear the Buddha Sing?" Excerpt from the Penguin publication, The Gift: Poems by Hafiz. Copyright © 1996 & 2003 by Daniel Ladinsky. Used and altered with his permission.

p. 86: Rumi, *"For years I gave away sexual love with my eyes. Now I don't."* "An Egypt that Doesn't Exist," <u>Open Secret: Versions of Rumi</u>, transl. John Moyne and Coleman Barks, Threshold Books, Putney, VT, 1984, p. 43

## CHAPTER 16 – RECOVERING FROM INFIDELITY: THE FOUR PILLARS

p. 89: John Lennon, "Woman"

p. 89: Johnny Cash, "I Walk the Line"

## CHAPTER 17 – THE SEXUAL DISCIPLINE OF THE MAR-RIED MAN

Some paragraphs of this chapter were originally published in the chapter "The Oaks of the Forest: In Praise of Discipline" in my book <u>How Long Till My Soul Gets It Right</u>? (Harper-Collins, 2001)

p. 93: Sienna Miller, from the film *Casanova*

p. 93: Rumi, "Praising Manners," <u>Night and Sleep</u>, Yellow Moon Press, Brighton, MA, 1981

p. 94: Rumi, *"Many have made the same mistake. . . . That's all."* <u>This Longing</u>, transl. Coleman Barks and John Moyne, Threshold Books, Putney, VT, 1988, Letter #24, p. 81

p. 96: St. Thèrése of Lisieux, *"Consider the oaks of the countryside, . . . and soon it attains a prodigious height."* <u>Collected Letters of St. Thèrése of Lisieux</u>, transl. F. J. Sheed., Sheed and Ward (an apostolate of the Priests of the Sacred Heart), Franklin, WI

## CHAPTER 18 – EIGHT DAYS A WEEK: THE DIMEN-SIONS OF MARITAL SEX

This chapter originally appeared in my book <u>How Long Till My Soul Gets It Right?</u> (HarperCollins, 2001) under the title "Eight Days a Week: Toward Great Sex in Marriage." I have revised it for this volume.

p. 99: Inanna, <u>Inanna: Queen of Heaven and Earth: Her Stories and Hymns from Sumer</u>, translated and edited by Diane Wolkstein and Samuel Noah Kramer, Harper and Row Publishers, NY, copyright © 1983 by Diane Wolkstein and Samuel Noah Kramer

p. 99: Ikkyu Sojun, "Song of the Dream Garden," in <u>The Erotic Spirit: An Anthology of Poems of Sensuality, Love, and Longing</u>, ed. Sam Hamill, Shambhala, Boston, 1996, p. 88

p. 101: Bhai Sahib, in <u>Chasm of Fire</u>, by Irina Tweedie, Element Publishers, Shaftesbury, Dorset, England, 1993, p. 91

p. 101: Walt Whitman, "We Two: How Long We Were Fooled"

p. 101: John Donne, "To His Mistress Going to Bed"

p. 102: Marvin Gaye, "Sexual Healing"

p. 103: James Joyce, <u>Chamber Music, #18</u>: "O Sweetheart, hear you Your Lover's tale," (1907), in <u>The Portable James Joyce,</u> Viking Press, New York, 1946, pp. 638-9

p. 104: Bob Dylan, "Shelter from the Storm"

p. 105: Indigo Girls, "Power of Two"

p. 105: Frankie Valli, "What a Night"

p. 106: The Traveling Wilburys, "It's a Dirty World"

p. 106: The Pointer Sisters, "I'm So Excited"

p. 107: Alice Walker, in <u>Women's Wicked Wisdom</u>, ed. Michelle Lovric, Chicago Review Press, Chicago, IL, 2003, p. 57

p. 108: John Mayer, "Your Body Is a Wonderland"

p. 108: k.d. lang, "The Air I Breathe"

p. 108: *"The true spiritual nature of love cannot be defined or described."* Narada, <u>Bhakti Sutras</u>. The <u>Bhakti Sutras</u> is a collection of 84 aphorisms on the nature of love written by the ancient sage Narada. The one quoted here is #51. The contemporary sage who explains the forms of love on earth is Swami Chidvilasananda, in a talk called *Believe in Love,* delivered on January 1, 2001 (SYDA Foundation, South Fallsburg, NY, CD #1, track 7).

## CHAPTER 19 – PLAN B: WHAT TO DO IF YOUR MARRIAGE ISN'T SEXY

p. 111: James Thurber, *"Is Sex Necessary?"* title of book written with E.B. White (1929)

p. 111: <u>Mundaka Upanishad</u>, Chapter 3. See the translations by Patrick Olivelle (<u>Upanishads</u>, Oxford University Press, 1996); Eknath Easwaran (<u>The Upanishads</u>, Nilgiri Press, 1987); Swami Prabhavananda and Frederick Manchester (<u>The Upanishads: Breath of the Eternal</u>, Vedanta Press, 1947); Juan Mascaró (<u>The Upanishads</u>, Penguin, 1965).

p. 112: *"The test of a first-rate intelligence is the ability to hold two opposed ideas in mind at the same time, and still retain the ability to function,"* F. Scott Fitzgerald, <u>The Crack-Up</u>

## CHAPTER 20 – LET'S GET IT ON

p. 119: Steve Miller Band, "The Joker"

p. 119: Rod Stewart, "Tonight's the Night"

p. 120: Marvin Gaye, "Let's Get It On"

## AFTERWORD: AN EARNEST APPEAL TO WIVES

p. 121: Brad Paisley, "I'm Still a Guy"

p. 121: Bob Dylan, "Lay, Lady, Lay"

CPSIA information can be obtained at www.ICGtesting.com
Printed in the USA
BVOW010201050213

312428BV00003B/10/P